TRUE COWBOY STORIES

TRAVIS W. HERRING

Travis Herring

ISBN:1-4610-9914-5

ISBN-13:978-1-4610-9914-7

CONTENTS

PROLOGUE

Dad said that he and Jesus Christ had something in common. When each were born, the fastest means of transportation was a horse and Dad lived to see man put on the moon. People had lived much the same for 2,000 years.

I was born in 1936 and lived on a large ranch 70 yards from my grand parents. Much of my early years were spent listening to Grandpa's stories of experiences on the Chisholm Trail and the old days. Brother in law John Nance and neighbor Jess Pickett was another source of first hand stories. Later, I ask other old timers for anything they remembered about them and other colorful characters. When I had children, I wrote the information down and gave my three kids a copy.

After I cut back on my ranching, I had a little extra time and decided to spend some of those cold winter days in 2009 digging out pictures and putting this information in book form.

I needed more pages, so I added the interesting story of how our home town of Lometa evolved from a stage stop to a steam engine stop. Also, the changes in farming and ranching with horses up to the present that I had a part in. Friends encouraged me to have it published. Enjoy!

CHAPTER ONE
LONG HORNS AND THE CHISHOLM TRAIL

William Joseph Herring was born in McLennan County in 1862 and later moved to Llano, Texas. As a young man, he went on a Longhorn cattle drive to Kansas. I loved to hear his stories of adventure on the trail.

(About the origin of the Longhorns) In 1521, calves were first brought to Mexico and Texas area from Santo Domingo, Spain. Twenty years later, Coronado left exhausted cattle on his exploration trip, thereby scattering the cattle in this area. Since the cattle had to survive the natural predators, they became as wild and wily as deer hiding in the thickets of the brush country. When they grazed or drank from streams, they were always on guard, nothing like the cattle of today. Thousands of Longhorn cattle were driven before and during the Civil War, but during the twenty odd years of the 1870s and 1880s, there was a conservative estimate of 10,000,000 head driven to the railhead in Kansas.

Like the wild mustang horses, the Longhorn cattle were there for the taking, but the taking was not easy. Many cattle were gentled down some, but most were not. Some were leaders that the rest of the herd followed in a long strung out line of two thousand or more head. It took cowboys to head the lead steers in the right direction, those on the sides, and the dust covered 'drag' boys on the rear. One seasoned older man was needed to scout out front for water and a place for the cattle to rest and graze. No feed was taken, so the cattle had to live off of the land on the trip. The saddle horses had to be rotated so they could rest and graze grass, too. The wrangler was in charge of the horses.

The worst obstacles were stampedes and water, or the lack of water, for such a huge number of cattle and horses. Their extraordinary wildness made them nervous and constantly alert of anything out of the ordinary. The most terrifying and common cause of stampedes was thunder and lightning. Grandpa Herring told about the static electricity that would play across the backs of the cattle, and how the cowboys became nervous when the Longhorns became nervous.

People could get killed by the cattle in a stampede and by their horse making a mistake in the darkness of unfamiliar country. Horses can see and sense things in the dark better than men, and some horses are better than others. The ones that were better at this were saved for night duty.

One story of a stampede that someone told, but that I am sure was stretched, was on the darkest of nights. The rider just gave his horse "his head "and had faith in him to see through the pitch black night. Soon after riding furiously at top speed, he felt as if he was falling through space for a long period of time. Finally, he hit the bottom and the horse just stood there shaking, and wouldn't move when the cowboy spurred him. The horse and rider stayed like that 'til daybreak when the cowboy looked down, and discovered why the horse wouldn't respond to the spurs. He was knee deep in solid rock.

W. J. told me of hardships such as stampedes in storms, crossing swelled rivers, and the cattle getting mixed with other herds—by the thousands. When this happened, it would take days to get all the proper brands with the right herd. Then, they might have to wait for the river to go down before they could attempt to cross. Most of the cattle drive bosses had to buy their way through Oklahoma Indian Territory by giving the Indians cattle before they could cross their range. This was much safer than fighting. Guess it was the prelude to a toll road. W. J. told of some of the cowboys and their wild days when they got to the railhead and loaded the cattle. A fellow he knew got in gunfight in a saloon and heard a woman scream after he shot. He was afraid that he had shot her by mistake. He high tailed it back to camp, got his belongings and left in a hurry and was never heard from again.

CHAPTER TWO
TRAIL HAND, JESS PICKETT

W. J. stayed up there in Kansas awhile and worked for the Southern Pacific railroad in the Devil River area. On the trail coming home, he and his pal were riding along and passed a farmhouse when a big cur dog ran out and tried to bite his foot. The owner of the dog was sitting on his porch watching the whole thing, Grandpa said. He jerked his foot up to keep from getting bitten and looked at the man. The man said nothing to his dog. The dog ran around to the other side of his horse and leaped up at his other foot. Grandpa jerked his foot up and looked at the man, who again said nothing to his dog. So, he took out his pistol and shot the dog dead. W. J. Herring had strong opinions about men and their responsibilities, even with their dog.

When he got back to Lometa, Texas, he went to see his old girlfriend in Llano. When he returned home, his dad asked how she was, and W. J. said she was married and had a kid. His dad said he was sorry to hear that. W. J. said, "Oh, that's alright, Dad. She was all suckled down and looked like hell."

W. J. had made close friends with a half-Negro by the name of Jess Pickett, (uncle of Bill Pickett, the inventor of Bull Dogging in rodeo) and they became close friends. Later, they bought ranches beside each other. People in this five-county area were real prejudiced to blacks back then, and there were no other black people around. Grandpa wanted Jess as a neighbor and being a real determined type person, said he would stand up for Jess and they would have to go through himself, if there was ever any opposition. Jess and W. J. continued to be close friends and neighbors until Jess died in 1943. Jess did more cattle buying and horse and mule trading, but W. J. was a breeder of horses and mules and cattle.

Jess was born to a Negro slave, and his father was Andy Mathews, her owner, an early day cowman, Indian fighter and scout. After Jess bought his ranch, his mother came and lived in a little house near Jess and his wife, Georgie. Aunt Silvia (1834-1916) as his mother was called, helped with the birth of my father at W. J.'s home. Aunt Silvia lived in a two-room cabin near Jess. For years, Aunt Silvia gathered up a wagonload of laundry in Lometa, washed it in a spring near her cabin, and then delivered it back to each house. When the "Eden Branch" railroad was being built, Jess brought her some large soft limestone rocks that had been blasted out of the right away. While the large limestone rocks were still damp and porous, she chiseled several water troughs out of them. After the limestone dries out, they become very hard. We still have them, along with other artifacts.

My dad, Fred Herring, told how Jess always had a rope in his hand and roped Dad's horses' legs, dogs, weeds, or any other target that caught his fancy. He didn't sling the rope around his head like most cowboys do when they are throwing the rope at a calf. The rope motions that other cowboys used would scare the calf, but Jess carried the rope on his shoulder and when the calf took his eyes off of him, then Jess would throw it in one motion, very fast. When the opportunity came—Sip!! The rope was on the calf. Once they were sorting calves on foot in the lot, and one got by that shouldn't. Jess threw over the six-foot fence and caught the calf running down the outside of the lot.

Jess was visiting at Grandpa's one day, still on his horse, and there was a shoat, a pig weighing approximately 170 pounds, walking around by the barn. Grandpa told Jess that he would give him the hog if he could load him on his horse by himself. Jess looked around, found a limb horizontal with the ground and herded the hog so that he was under it.. He threw the rope over the limb, caught the head and one fore leg (as necessary since hogs don't have a neck) pulled him up, circled the tree and set the hog in front of the saddle and rode off with his hog without saying a word. Grandpa said, "I just stood there with my mouth open."

Jess rode with North Longfield, Hustutlers, and other cattle traderes on cattle buying trips. They would usually stay overnight near a farm in order to use their water, or shed if bad weather, and sometimes buy some grain for their horses. Once when they were asking permission to stay and told the farmer that they had a black man with them. Some people in the area would not let a black man on their property. The farmer said, "Yeah, I noticed" and pointed to the wrong man! Jess couldn't let his friend forget the farmer's mistake.

During another trip they were in their bedrolls trying to get that last bit of sleep before getting up, and a turkey gobbler kept strutting and dragging his wing feathers on the ground between their bedrolls. Jess lost his temper and grabbed the turkey by the neck, but just then he saw the farmer come out of the house, so he pitched the flopping turkey under the Englishman's bedroll. In his English brogue, he shouted, "Jess, there is something in the bed with me!" Grandpa really enjoyed telling that story.

M. F. Klose's grandfather, Charlie, told me about a mule trade with Jess. After they closed the deal with a handshake, Mr. Klose said, "OK, Jess, now tell me. What is wrong with my mule?" Jess told him he thought that he was an 'outlaw' and would never be able to break him. He said, "You had better set the plow deep and have a big stout mule on either side." Mr. Klose, also a horse and mule trader, said, "Yours has bad lungs and is useless." Later, they met in town and Mr. Klose asked Jess what did he do with that mule he swapped him. He told him that he sold him! Mr. Klose said, "I want to hear how you did it." Jess said he had a buyer coming at a certain time, so he hooked the mule to the cultivator and made one round in the field. He told me that people normally used their best mule to pull the cultivator because it only took one and they didn't want to plow up the little corn plants. After that one round, the mule was sweating and gasping for air. He tied him by the yard fence gate and when the buyer came, the mule was wet with sweat like he had been plowing all day, but was breathing normal. Jess said he and the buyer started walking to the mule pen, but the buyer kept looking back at my cultivator mule. Finally, he said he just had to have my cultivator mule, so I let him have him.

Jess had a neighbor and friend that was very tight with his money and never donated any thing for the community. As Jess was going to town for a community Bar B Q to raise money, he noticed one of the old tightwad's goats out in the lane. So, Jess roped the goat, took it in and told them that the old man had donated the goat for the Bar B Q.

Jess and Georgie couldn't have kids, and they had more of everything than they ever needed, so they were good about helping others. I heard many an old timer tell about how Jess and Georgie had helped others during the Great Depression. Jess would tell the grocery man to take food out to a family and not tell them who sent it. He didn't want them to feel obligated to him. Dad talked about an old friend he grew up with who became an oil executive in Midland, Texas, that said he would not be where he was if Jess hadn't loaned him the money to go to college. Jess had a good friend, a white man whom he liked, who was in financial distress and needed $2,500 at once. That was a lot of money back then. He appealed to Jess, and Jess said no, that he didn't have it handy, but said he knew where he could get it. He told him to go to Mr. John Brandon tomorrow and said I think he'll let you have it. Jess then hurried to Mr. Brandon, gave him the $2,500, and told him that the neighbor would soon be asking for a loan in that amount. "Let him have this money," said Jess, "but never let him know it came from me". I know the loan is good, but I must keep out of it." Puzzled at this, Brandon asked him why the secrecy. Jess said, "This man is my friend. He doesn't realize it now, but if I let him have the money, the day may come when he would be ashamed of himself for having to borrow money from a nigger, and he would come to hate me. I don't want that to happen. It's better to handle it like this."

Since Jess and Georgie couldn't have children, and Grandpa and Grandma were too old, so Jess kept after my dad that it was time to have some babies. He told my dad, here we have these two good sized ranches with baby sheep, goats, horses and cattle, but no babies. It was during the Great Depression, and dad told him he couldn't afford kids. Jess said, "You have them, and I'll pay for them." He paid the doctor's and hospital bills on both my sister and I. Jess came to see us nearly every day. He would come by the house early in the morning around breakfast time, and sometimes with a straight face he would say, "I've come to foreclose—I want my kids." Then he would take us to Lometa, and get us a soda pop. This is the one reason that I have included so much about Jess. He was like a godfather to me.

Jess Pickett with my sister and I

At Jess's funeral, the white Baptist preacher from Lometa did the honors, and all of the pallbearers were white. They were mostly ranchers, and more than one of them had, at times, borrowed money from Jess. Jess was about 68 or 69 when he died. Fred Herring bought the Pickett ranch, and Georgia lived another 20 years in Lometa with the Herring family looking after her.

CHAPTER THREE
BILL PICKETT, BULL DOGGER

Jess had a nephew who grew up in the same area, near Taylor, Texas, by the name of Bill Pickett.

Bill learned his bull dogging rodeo technique by watching bulldogs that retrieved wandering livestock by locking onto the bigger animals' lips with their teeth. The 5'7", 145 pound Pickett didn't use his muscular arms and strong hands to twist down a steer by its horns and nose as they do today on the rodeo circuit. Bill would ride out of the starter gate, fling himself out of the saddle onto the head of a running steer, grab its horns, and pull its head up. Digging into the dirt with his heels to slow the animal, Bill would lean down, grab the steer's upper lip with his teeth, and sink them into the tender flesh. The steer, wild with pain, slowed to a stop as Bill turned the horns loose and threw both hands into the air to show that he held the steer with only his teeth.

The Dusty Demon, as some called him, performed at Wyoming's Cheyenne Frontier Days, the World's Fair, Madison Square Garden, the 101 Ranch Wild West Show and many other places. The show had cowboys like Tom Mix, Hoot Gibson, Will Rogers, and the great Apache chief, Geronimo, but it was Bill Pickett who remained the show's biggest attraction. The Great Depression caused the Wild West Show to close in 1931. After breaking many bones in his profession, the next year he was separating horses in a coral, and one horse reared up and pawed him in the head and killed Bill. His friend, humorist Will Rogers, who some claim once served as a hazer who kept steers in line for Pickett, eulogized his old friend on his nationwide radio show. "Bill Pickett never had an enemy," Rogers said, "Even the steers wouldn't really hurt old Bill."

Forty years after his death, Bill Pickett was honored as the first black cowboy to be inducted into the National Rodeo Hall of Fame in Oklahoma City. A larger than life statue of Bill bulldogging a Longhorn steer is located on the main street of the old stockyards in Fort Worth, Texas.

CHAPTER FOUR
BACHELOR COWBOY WHITT COBLE

Will, Whitt, Coble was a bachelar cowboy all of his life. He was a little younger than Jess Pickett, so I knew him a little longer but not as well. His niece, Mrs. Quince Stone, told me a little more about her uncle Will and his Dad. His dad had a blacksmith shop in Senterfitt, West of where Lometa would be later established. He shod horses and taught Whitt the trade as well as breaking horses. Whitt was a typical cowboy with high topped riding bots, hat and denim clothing. He fought in World War I and the worst thing he said was wearing their Army boots. He said they ruined his feet.

A farmer near Senterfitt had been plowing for the public and driving his team of mules to and from work everyday, to feed and care for them at night. He probably had been walking behind a plow all day, too. He saw Whitt braking horses one day and ask him if he would break one of his mules so that he could ride to work.

One time, he was working on a round up in West Texas and came in to the chuck wagon for a meal. He said a little too much to the cook while he was mixing biscuits to put in the Dutch oven on the open fire. Most chuck wagon cooks are a little cranky, as this one apparently was, but he said nothing. There was a sack of horse feed oats with their rough husks sitting near the wagon. Whitt said the old man just got a hand full of those oats and mixed it with my biscuits.

When Whitt was up in years, it was said some lady gave him the receipt to a cake that he really thought was good. He decided he was going to cook it and he lay the receipt out on the table, got his glasses and read, take one CLEAN bowel. That was as for as he could go.

In about 1950, Fort Hood had one of the largest army maneuvers in the Lometa area. There were troop trains and truck loads of soldiers in and out of Lometa for several weeks. My mother and several other ladies opened a café on rail road street to serve home cooking to the boys. They had women all over bringing in cakes and pies. The soldiers wouldn't just buy a piece of pie, they bought the whole thing.

After school, when I could, I would help the ladies, because it was the busiest time of the day. One day, a yankee soldier was telling me that Texas just wasn't what he thought it would be. He saw the ranchers pickup with a gun and cow prod on a rack behind the seats, and cow dogs in the back-but he didn't see them riding in on a horse. About that time, Whitt Coble came walking in with his bowed legs and his spurs jingling- his high toped boots and tall hat, Levi shirt. The Yankee's mouth was open, he swiveled on his stool as he went by and he said "there is the real Mc Coy!". I said "yes, he is."

CHAPTER FIVE

COWBOY BILL LEWIS

Bill Lewis was another colorful cowboy that I knew that was just a little older than myself. He looked the part with the knee high boots with pants legs tucked in, denim clothes and uncreased black hat, but he really was a cowboy!

He had only worked horse back for cowmen. His nephew Troy Van Cleave, told me several stories, one of which he told his new employer that he was no Mexican and only worked from horse back. After several days, his boss told him to tie stay posts into a fence. Stays are small posts tied to each wire from top to bottom to make the fence stronger. After a couple of days the boss came to check on him and all the stays were 'only' tied at the top of the post to the top wire. He ask Bill why. And Bill reminded him of their agreement that he only worked from horse back.

This same boss was a wealthy lawyer that was a little tight with his money. The Animal Rights people demanded that he feed those poor cows! So, he told Bill that a big truck was coming that morning and he wanted it all dumped in one big pile. Bill told him the cows were so hungry that they would over eat, but he said "do it!" Sure enough, the next morning Bill went to see the cows and many were found "quarto pala arriba"- Four feet up. The Animal Rights people didn't come back again.

This boss man tore off a piece of a paper feed bag and wrote a note for the bank to give Bill ten dollars for supplies. The teller at the bank sent him to the president. He knew how tight the boss was and ask him if he had been paying him his full salary. So, the banker gave him the ten dollars plus his salary.

Another time the boss sent him to check on another ranch that several citizens from deep in Mexico were taking care of. There were several dead cows. It was extra cold that part of the winter and these men were not accustomed to working in it and how to take care of the cows under those conditions. Bill asked them if they had chopped the ice on the ponds, so they could drink the water, and they said "Oh yes, once, but it just froze over again!"

Bill's daughter, Sandra Baskin, told about his last employer, Thomas Earl Winters and his brother in law Billy Bob, established the famed dance hall in Fort Worth old Stockyards area, "Billy Bob's" The largest Honky Tonk in the world. He took Bill off the ranch with his horse and went to the big city! For publicity, he had Bill ride his horse into the lobby of the Union Tower in downtown Fort Worth, blind fold the horse and ride him up the elevator to the top floor. When he arrived and the doors opened, there was a big wig banquet going on. So, they joined in with the festivities. Horses like beer, too. He was used to parties, because he rode the horse and was the last chance bouncer at Billy Bob's. If some ole boy got unruly, Bill roped him and dragged him out like he would have done a calf.

Talking about dragging, not too long after he was married, he had an old pickup that sometimes he had to drag it to get it rolling, then jump off his horse, get in the pickup and throw it in gear to get it started. His wife said that she thought that was dangerous, so she agreed to sit in the pickup while Bill pulled it with his horse. When he got it to rolling good, she pumped the gas pedal and put it in gear as instructed. The truck started with a leap, but she was not accustomed to the gears and passed him up and jerked the horse down on top of poor Bill.

Life is tuff in the country! Thomas Earl, his boss, came out to see the guys working on a windmill, when something broke and the windmill fell and cut off his foot. Bill had a wreck with a neighbor, Dutch Smith, and a year or so later had a head on with my wife. Some one told him, Bill, your neighbors or going to kill you!" I took them to the hospital in Lampasas and was as worried about Bill as I was my wife. He had been very quiet all the twenty miles to the hospital and holding his stomach. He was in an emergency room next to Mary's when I heard him tell the doctor "hell I can't stay here. I have to go drench some sheep!" I quit worrying about Bill. His boy was in my Agriculture class at the Lometa school, and he said "Mr. Herring, you know that old dog that used to ride every where with dad in the back of the pickup?" He said, "he won't ride with him any more!." My friends Bill and Thomas Earl have passed on from this world. Both from natural causes.

CHAPTER SIX
COWBOYS - COWMEN WITTENBURGS AND GIBSONS

Gibsons moved to the Bend area on the Colorado river in 1856 and have kept the farm and ranch in the family ever since. In the mid to late 1950's, Foy was working with Troy Pope trying to round up Pope's cattle. The cattle had gotten on Gibson land and Pope didn't have pens to catch them in. There were thick post oak canopies with shin oak under growth along with other low ground cover shrubs. This was normal terrain in those days in this hill and bush country part of Texas. As they were gathering the cattle there near the river, a cow Foy was trying to turn wheeled and hooked the horse in the right shoulder. If Foy had not raised his leg in the stirrups, she would have gored his leg. The cow's horn went underneath it and hooked the horse, driving her horn into him leaving an ugly hole almost killing the horse. He got off and led him back to the pen and got on another and went back to finish the job. Later, he loaded the injured horse and had him treated at the Veterinary. The horse turned out alright and continued to work as a cow horse for several more years.

A similar incidence, with another cowboy chasing cows, ran into a broken dead limb and it went into the cowboys side like a spear. He went to the hospital and lived to cowboy again.

Foy Gibson was cowboying down on Lemon's camp near Sulfur Spring along the river doctoring screw worms in cattle back in the 1940's. They even roped young deer when they found one and doctored them in the navel area to keep them from being infested.   One day, he spooked a bunch of wild hogs causing his horse to throw him. The hogs attacked him and bit him in the thigh and shredded his pants leg. He wore out his hat whooping the hogs off. Luckily, the horse didn't run away, and after beating the hogs off he was able to get back on his horse and get home. He didn't go to the doctor, but cleaned and fixed up his own leg. He had on loose fitting pants so it ripped them more than it did his legs. As for as his hat was concerned, he said it was in pretty bad shape to begin with.

Later on, in his older years, he graduated to a four -wheeler to chase cows. In about 1988, they were penning calves close to dark, and he tried to turn some large 700 pound calves. They didn't turn. The cattle hit the four-wheeler and all anyone could see through the dust was tail lights and head lights in the air. They thought for sure he was dead or injured, but when they found him, he was alright but the four- wheeler was upside down.

William Mark Wittenburg left Germany for America in 1848 and finally settled in our area of Texas Hill Country in 1879. Son Joseph Morgan and daughter Ida who married Kirk Buttrill have children here today. They became one of the largest land owners in this area and it was populated with a lot of Wittenburgs. Good friend Joe Wittenburg shared the following stories: Following the Civil War, in the absence of the protection of law, many people had their barns burned and livestock stolen. Once when William Mark Wittenburg was returning home he was met by several of his neighbors who informed him that his barn had been burned and they had been unable to save it. They weren't surprised when he said "The Lord giveth and the Lord taketh away". "But damn the SOB's who burned my barn."

Joe's aunt Ida Wittenburg Butrell was on a trip in West Texas with strong headed Ida driving and Uncle Kirk riding shot gun. Kirk was looking at the map and stated that the next town was Balmorhea. Aunt Ida said "no, it is Saragosa." Kirk looked at the map again and said it was Balmorhea. Ida said Saragosa. After studying the map one more time, he rolled down the window and threw the map out the window. Ida said in a very disturbed voice, "what did you do that for?" Kirk said "the damn thing was wrong."

CHAPTER SEVEN
COWBOY-COWMAN W. J. HERRING

W. J. married Ella Miller in 1890. At that time, his brand spelled his name on the side of the cow with the letters HER with a circle around it. The circle represented a RING, completing the Herring name. The ring around it prevented rustlers from changing his brand. (No, he didn't put it on his new wife) When his old lifetime companion and neighbor Jess Pickett died, son Fred Herring bought his ranch and soon afterward he and his son, Travis, registered Pickett's brand in their name in remembrance of Jess. At that time, there was very little brand changing by rustlers, and it didn't affect much of the hide since we put it high on the left hip a few inches in front of the tail head. All cattle on the two ranches and leased ranches have been fire branded like this ever since 1962. When Travis Herring came back to ranch with Fred Herring, Travis registered the 'Flying V' brand that had been used by Jess Pickett. The 'Flying V' was painted on the Pickett's water storage tank. In later years, Kleburgh Agriculture Building at Texas A&M was completed, and someone from each county in the state of Texas was asked to bring a brand to be burned into the wall next to the staircase. Travis Herring took the branding iron for the Flying V to represent Lampasas County.

Besides farming and ranching with mules and horses, W. J. had another livelihood. He was a breeder of horses and mules.

In 1540, the Coronado Expedition brought horses from Spain into the Southwest part of our country and many were lost or stolen by the Indians. The most hardy were the horses that lived to multiply. This strengthened the hardiness of the Arabian-Barb breeding. Among the finest Arabian horses one may see black mane and tails and occasionally a suggestion of a dorsal stripe. The name Mustang came from the Spanish word, Mestenas, which means wild, unbranded and ownerless. The most familiar color with the original horse was a dun with a dark stripe down the spine. Both Arabian and thoroughbred breeders have tried to breed it out, but it is prevalent in the Spanish horse and most old time cowboys will say the wider the stripe, the tougher the horse. Most were smaller than horses used on ranches today. Many old ranchers say, "There is no breeder like a scrub among man or beast." The Mustang was hardy, tough and adapted to the life, but with short pasterns and legs, he was very rough riding. Through selection in breeding came better Mustangs, but most of the advancement came through the introduction of other breeds from other countries. Even the favorite horse for cowboys, the Quarter Horse, was developed in my generation.

Since the horses and mules were the trucks and tractors of the day, there was a good demand for them. W. J. had a jack, a male donkey, that he serviced customer's mares, a female horse, to deliver the hybrid mule. I remember seeing the breeding stanchion where they led the mare 'down' into it, so the shorter jack could reach her.

Sometimes a customer would bring his mare to be bred by his big horse, the stallion, and then, sometimes he would ride to the customers' house to service the mare. To convince them of how gentle the stallion was, Dad said that Grandpa would pitch him up on the stud when he was only two or three years old.

Grandpa sat on the front porch of his colonial style house when he was old and lame. I had to open a gate by his porch every time I crossed the road with my horse. Grandpa would yell, "Pull that horse's head around to you when you mount!" I paid him no mind, and just 'climbed' back on my horse each time. But years later when I broke my first colt, I discovered what he meant. When a rider steps into the stirrup with his left foot and goes to swing his right leg over the horse and saddle, it is natural for the horse to move to the right away from the rider. Thus, he has to pull the horse's head to him as he goes to mount. Instead of being a chore getting into the saddle, the rider just raises his right leg and the horse turns into it making for a more effortless mount even for a well-trained horse. Then, I saw what Grand pa was talking about. Other advice, was to take a deep seat. Instead of standing tall in the stirrups, as a movie cowboy does, to look good, it is best to work or ride in the pastures with one's legs a little out front sitting back in the saddle seat. One time I was riding along with out a worry in the world, and my horse nearly dropped out from under me and backed up at the same time. My body and arms moved forward automatically and the reins wound up on one side of his neck. The horse had nearly stepped on a huge coiled rattlesnake. If I had not had a 'deep seat', I would have probably been dropped on the snake.

Everything in the design of the cowboy riding boot is for a purpose.

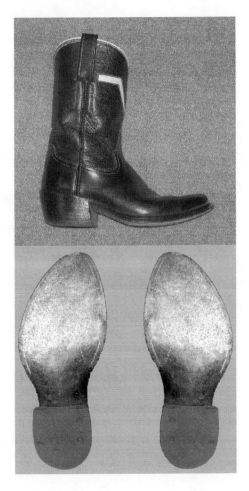

Remember that the cowboy spent most of his time either in the saddle or getting on and off to open gates, doctor calves or other reasons. The pointed toe made it easier to hit the stirrup if he was in a hurry or the horse was. With a tall horse and a smaller cowboy, he had to hit it as he jumped. If the toe was out front in the middle of the toes, it would hang in bushes or tree limbs, therefore, the design was a fairly straight line on the inside of the boot. The entire boot, from heal to toe lay flat against the horse with a slope from the pointed toe angling to the outside to shed the brush around and off the end of the boot.

The heel was tall or long so it was a "stop" on the stirrup to keep the entire foot from going through if the horse fell or the rider lost his seat. Most horses are terrified when something is dragging. Many a rider has been seriously hurt being dragged and quite a few killed. I knew a man that didn't have any hair growing on the back side of his head after once being dragged a long distance back to the barn.

The tall heel, two inches or so, needed to be slopping in, from the back. The reason being, the tendency to drag and wear out the back portion of the heal while walking. The sole of the boot needs to hit the ground about the same time as the heel. This also lessens the appearance of the heel being so tall. Hence, the term long tall Texan.

The leather of the foot over laps the leg tops in the front to keep it from wearing out as fast rubbing against the stirrup. Extra layers of leather are added to the heel to support the spurs. That over lap of foot leather in front, also cushions the pressure of the spur strap and buckle. The high tops protect the legs and ankles when the pants work up in the sitting position, especially important here in the hill and brush country. Our country has a significant population of diamond back rattle snakes. This alone, is a good reason for the boot tops. Some say, that is why they ride a horse instead of walking. There is no muscle below the knee of the horse for the snake to bite into. Only bone and tendon with few blood vessels.

Some cowboys have different colorful stitching on the tops and some have bright colored leather. Personally, my tops are the same color as the bottom and only have a white inlay of my flying V brand. Recent years, as many have quit riding horseback, the design has moderated to shorter heels and round toes like shoes. The phrase, "he died with his boots on", was a true and frequent statement. Cowboying was and still is a dangerous job.

CHAPTER EIGHT
SCREW WORMS-PLAGUE OF THE RANCHER

Until, 1960, livestock raisers lost a large percentage of their offspring in the spring and summer from the screwworm flies. The temperatures of the first frost would kill the screwworm flies for the season. After the last frost in the spring, the screwworm would become active again. The fly would lay its eggs on a damp spot, any damp spot like the navel of a newborn, a watering eye, or the rear end. Within a week, the animal would have a case of worms eating into live flesh. The difference between the maggot and the screwworm is that the maggot only eats dead tissue. The screwworm would eat only live flesh and multiply so fast that the poor animal wouldn't last long. The rancher could save the animal if he caught, doctored and watched him in his hospital pasture until the animal was healed and the wound dried up. Finding the infected animals and working your hospital pasture like a good doctor or nurse was a confining job. Many wounds were horrible looking, worse than anything you have seen on television, and the animals were still alive and in pain. If they looked this bad, we put them out of their misery, usually with a .22 bullet.

For this reason, the ranchers would ride horseback many hours every day, or at least every other day. Half of the Herring's 1800-acre ranch is on a mountain that was brushy with rocks larger than a car in many places on the sides of the mountain. Especially the goats would be found between the cracks of rocks or caught under the overhangs of the rocks trying to get away from the flies. One would have to get off the horse to find them, being careful not to get bitten by a rattlesnake. I remember one time when I was probably about eight years old, Dad sent me in one place between the rocks with a small opening to look for wormies. There was a mother buzzard with a nest of babies in the back of the slit between the rocks. When we met, she was just as afraid as I was, and she was trying to fly past me beating me with her wings. I don't know which one of us made it out first or which one was the most terrified, but my Dad nearly fell off his horse laughing. To this day, I still believe he knew she was in there.

It was best to find the wormies, as we called the goats carrying the worms, before they went into hiding. I have spent many hours sitting on my horse, just watching a herd of cows or a flock of goats looking for a sign. The wormies would tend to bite at the wound. It probably tickled the goat at first causing them to shake their head or rear end. That's what I watched for. Usually, we would rope the goat and doctor it, but if the wound was bad, we carried the goat on horseback to the hospital pasture. We would drive the cow and calf back to the pens to doctor it. The more you rode, the more you saved. There were no weekend ranchers from the city back then. They couldn't have raised any, or many, offspring and therefore made any profit. The demand for cow horses was still good, even though the pickup truck replaced many good cow horses.

CHAPTER NINE
BREAKING HORSES

Grandpa gave his two sons, Loyd and Fred, the barely broke broncs to ride to school for more training –sons and horses. Theirs and other kids were always having accidents or being bucked off. Dad told me of one horse that always wanted to run, so one day going to school, he turned him loose. When he came over the hill north of Lometa by the graveyard "running ninety to nothing", he met a lady in a one-horse buggy. Trying to stop or turn the bronc, he hit the buggy and turned it over. It didn't hurt the lady, but it sure made her angry! Dad laughed as he told me that she was fussing about these wild young drivers. My old farrier, the man who shoed the horses, Truit Holiday, told me about my mother's brother, Rex Ivey, while he was shoeing my horse, Red # 1

Mr. Holiday had a blacksmith shop downtown and heard a horse in a full run coming from the direction of the school. He walked out to see the commotion, and there was a horse, saddled with the reins blowing in the wind, but with no rider. He laughed and went back into the shop. Then there came the sound of a person running down the street in the same direction of the horse. Later, hearing the sound of a horse in full run again, he went out to see Rex in the saddle whipping and spurring the horse. Rex quit school some time later and moved to the wildest part of Texas, the Big Bend. It matched his personality, but Uncle Rex is altogether a different story.

CHAPTER TEN
HORSE RACING

Ranchers and cowboys liked to brag on how fast their horses were. Sometimes, it's put your money where your mouth is, and it called for a race. Usually, there had been talk around town enough to get a lot of others into the discussion, so there would be a little betting on the horses. It might be a long fifteen or twenty mile race or a short sprint.

Old timers were still talking about a little old bent man that rode into town one day on a horse that didn't look in much better condition that his rider. The horse even had a slight limp on one leg. The old man was modestly bragging on the horse, and finally got a lot of people betting him that he couldn't out run Jake's horse. After stirring up the crowd, there was a lot of money bet against the stranger's horse, and the stranger was the only one betting on his horse. The old timers are still talking about how the looks and attitude of that old crippled horse changed when they lined up to start the race. It was no contest! And the stranger left with pockets full of money headed for another small town.

The Lampasas-Dallas Marathon was held in 1936 in observance of the 100th anniversary of Texas Independence from Mexico.

Participants rode on horseback, the distance between the Lampasas County Courthouse and the gates of the Centennial Exposition in Dallas. D. A. 'Leck' Roberts, with Hazel, is pictured on the sidewalk in Lampasas after winning the race.

"The prize was five hundred dollars, a Texas Centennial saddle, and a pair of boots given to him by the store, Cox and Shanks. Back then, five hundred dollars would have bought 200 acres of land.

For speed and distance, Francois Xavier Aubrey was tops in the whole riding tradition of the West. He was five foot two and weighed a little over one hundred pounds, but his body was distilled energy. He prospered as a trader hauling freight from Independence, Missouri to Santa Fe, New Mexico. In 1848, the trip on horseback took three to four weeks to ride the eight hundred miles. Mr. Aubrey announced that he would make the trip in six days, and the bets ran high.

Mr. Aubrey sent men ahead to have horses in readiness at different places. It was to be a lone ride over an empty land. He left Santa Fe on September the twelfth and ate only six meals on the ground, stopped only once to sleep for two hours before his final New Mexican horse stopped at Independence, Missouri. He ate a little while riding, and after the first day and night out, he tied himself to the saddle so that he could doze without fear of falling off. The horse would follow the freight trail even though the rider was asleep. After the gait was set, a good horse would keep it by himself. At "Point of Rocks", the relay man holding the next horse had been killed by Indians and the horse stolen. Aubrey was riding his favorite yellow mare, a Spanish dun named Dolly. On and on she went until she carried Aubrey two hundred miles in twenty-six hours. Buffalo Bill had said that fifteen miles an hour speed on horseback will in time shake a man to pieces. Aubrey was made of rawhide.

Back in the early 1930's when Seabiscuit was born, was during the terrible Great Depression time of America's history. Just about every one was poor and with no hope. Charles Howard had bought Seabiscuit even though he was too small, short, and gave him a trainer that was too old and later a jockey that was too large.

Everything seemed to be against him and the public could relate to that. They came in huge numbers to see and boost him on as he raced against all odds. The trainer, Tom Smith, was a real cowboy in his early years and he knew horses and could do things with them that other trainers couldn't. He was at least one of the first "Horse Whisperers". He found that Seabiscuit didn't run well if he didn't want to. So, Tom taught him to enjoy staying ahead of the other horses. The horse came to love him.

George Woof was the jockey that rode him the most years. Like Seabiscuit, he had an independent personality, but they got along very well. Years later, George was killed riding another horse when he fell racing over forty miles per hour.

Seabiscuit had an injury that caused him to stop all training for a full year, and when he came back to race, everyone thought he was too old. After beating all the odds during his younger years, his followers were behind him but afraid he would hurt him self again. He ran a photo finish with the son of "Man of War" and went on to win the World Championship.

CHAPTER ELEVEN
STORIES OF LIFE IN THE OLD DAYS

Uncle John Nance and W. J.'s sister, Aunt Josie, lived in Lometa. Their house is still standing (2010). When I was a small kid, they came out to the ranch a lot, and I loved to hear them talk of the old days. Once Grandpa and Uncle John got to discussing an old quarrel they had when John was bragging about his new car and Grandpa was taking up for his horses. These automobiles were cutting into his horse business. Grandpa had challenged John's new car to a duel for power with his big stallion. They had tied a rope on the bumper of the car, and Grandpa took a dally of the rope on his saddle horn and then jabbed the spurs to his stud. John was laughing saying, "I beat you, too." Grandpa said, "You wouldn't have if your tire hadn't caught in those live oak tree roots and my saddle girt hadn't broken."

John Nance was a squirrel hunter, and W. J. was a deer hunter. They had many tales about their dogs and hunts. Grandpa told his boys that they couldn't all be deer hunters because of the ranch work. "There can only be one, and I am it." He hunted horseback with a 12-gauge pump shot gun, or when on foot, he used a long-barrel 1894 Winchester lever action 30-30. Of course, the big thing about deer hunting, or any kind of hunting, is the camping out and the fun you have with your buddies around a campfire.

There were no deer near here at that time, so you had to go somewhere else to hunt. When he got old and crippled up, the younger guys would put 'Uncle Will' on a hill where he could see a long way, then come back at the end of the day and pick him up. His old '94 special would shoot further than the short barrel rifles, and Grandpa was a good shot, so he usually got a deer to provide meat for the family.

Two fellows got to arguing about who was the best shot, so they decided to use their hats as targets. The first threw his hat in the air, and the other followed it in his sights and shot one round and missed. Then, they reversed. The other man followed his hat in his sights as it went up and came down, then blew a hole in the hat after it hit the ground. A bigger argument followed.

At this time, there were no deer with in 50 miles of Lometa, unlike there are now, and deer hunters had to go to Llano, Texas, or further. There were plenty of squirrels in our area, so Uncle John didn't have to go far with his dog and .22 target rifle. The squirrel would crawl around to the backside of the tree, keeping the tree trunk as cover between him and the hunter, therefore the use of the squirrel dog was useful. John used a Fox Terrier to circle around the tree and bring the squirrels into view. After Uncle John died, Aunt Josie was saying she sure missed eating squirrel. So, as a boy who liked to hunt, too, I kept her in squirrels from then on.

Grandpa allowed himself another pleasure by going to town for a shave everyday. It was a bigger job back when you had to use a straightedge blade, and it was a large part of the income of barbers back then. Of course, Grandpa would go to the café for coffee and the local news. One old timer told me that Grandpa left his quirt (that he used on his horse) hanging on his wrist, sometimes. He liked kids, and he would test the little boys spirit by swatting them on the behind when they walked by. If they bowed up to him, he got a big kick out of it. He admired a horse, or a boy, with a little spirit!

Which reminds me of a Sunday afternoon when my three older cousins from Lampasas were visiting and, as a three year old, I was going to show them how brave I was, and I spit on a big nest of red wasps. Well, you can guess what happened. They stung me all over the face! For days, every time I would walk across the road to see Grandpa and Grandma, Grandpa would ask me if I had been spitting on any more wasp nests. Then, he would die laughing. One day, I had had enough. I marched right by him into the kitchen and got as a large a piece of cook stove firewood that I could handle. While he had the newspaper up and couldn't see me, I whacked him as hard as I could on the shins. May be that he was testing my spirit.

Mick Stephens told me this story: The road through the Herring ranch was the main road from Goldthwaite west and to Lampasas south until the State Highway 183 was built. Grandpa loved to talk to travelers (when he had time) when they stopped by his water trough. He had put one in front of the house for their use. He told me about the time the circus came by and all the elephants and animals watered. Nearly used up all the water that the windmill had put in his storage tank. During the planning stage of the proposed highway 183, W. J. got an appointment with the governor of Texas at the capital. Well, he said, "Governor, you know there is bound to be some money under the table on building this 183 highway deal!" The governor said, "Now, Mr. Herring, have you seen the money." Grandpa said, "HELL NO!! I haven't seen New York City, but I know it's there!!" The following is not a quote from Grandpa, but it sounds like him: 'When listening to a politician, one has to wade through a lot of crap to get to the bottom line. And all politicians don't work for the government.'

Grandpa believed very strongly about what is right. He put his money where his mouth is, too. He was a bank director at the Lometa bank when it failed in the 1930s, and all of the directors but Grandpa and one other director said it was not their fault, and they didn't pay. Grandpa sold cattle and some land to pay his part of the bank losses. He taught me a lot of things, but he stressed that your name is the most important thing you have. As a boy, I grew up wanting to be a good horse man and cow man like him, but the one thing I couldn't be was as tall as him. He and my dad worked the ranch together all of Dad's life as I did with my dad. Grandpa died when I was 14 at the age of 89 years.

When I was pre-school age, Mother would let me walk the hundred yards across the road to Grandma and Grandpa's house.

Cars were not all that fast in the 1930s, she wasn't afraid of me getting run over. I would pick wild flowers on the way for Grandma, play checkers with Grandpa, and listen to cowboy stories of his younger days. I took their advice and preaching much better than from my folks. It was God, country, family, and Will Rogers. A man's reputation and word is the most important thing he has control over. He was a bank director and later my dad. I did chores and started a bank account at their urging before I was old enough to go to school. Once we were in Lampasas, the county seat, and I gave a check for something and the storekeeper wouldn't take it because I was so young. When I walked back to the car and told Grandpa, he went back in and chewed the guy out. Most people in the county knew him.

My sister and I had a guard dog, Fritz, a big German shepherd. There were lots of rattle snakes in the grass in the summer, and Fritz could be counted on to stay in front of us no matter which way we turned. Mother didn't worry as long as he was with us because he would kill the snakes on the spot. When our four cousins from Lampasas would come for Sunday dinner, Fritz took care of us. He also knew when to line up with us for photos, and would sit down and smile from ear to ear. He is in all our kid pictures.

When I was told that I had to go to school (at six years of age), I told them that I couldn't go. I had to help my dad ranch. I had been on a horse following Dad's horse looking for wormies since I was a kid! Some times, I would go to sleep riding, and Dad would catch hold of a limb and swat me with it to wake me. Well, that first school day when I started to get on the school bus, my big Fritz came on, too. The driver was afraid of him, but persuaded me into talking Fritz off the bus.

I always loved raising baby animals, and we had a mother cat that did, too. When she had kittens, I would steal a baby squirrel or rabbit out of their nest and give it to her. She would mother it like it was her very own. One spring, Papa Ivey brought us two little black animals so small that they didn't have their eyes open yet. He had no idea what they were, and my sister and I asked friends whose dads hunted with hound dogs to come tell us what the animals were. No one knew. The mama cat loved them just the same. After about two months, they begin to turn a little gray, except for down their back, and their heads grew longer and narrower. Finally, Dad said they were gray foxes! They were house broke and were raised in the house and thought that they were part of the family. One day Dad had a man visiting on business, and as they were talking in the living room, the door was open to my sister's bedroom with one of the nearly grown foxes lying between the pillows on her bed. The man was facing that room when dad noticed the frozen expression on the man's face. Dad looked to where he was looking, and the fox had stood up and stretched. The man probably thought it was a fur until the fox stood up on the bed.

Dad made little harnesses and a leash for the two fox and took us to a pet show at the Hostess House in Lampasas. I was about eight years old. Turned out, it really was a dog show and another one of Dad's pranks. I lead the foxes up the stairs, or they lead me eagerly, and when we got to the room full of dogs of all kinds, you should have seen and heard it! The pair of fox was innocent because they were raised around dogs and cats, but the dogs in the show thought they were wild predators. The people and their dogs were wild with excitement, shouting and barking. Maybe now, you can see why so many people, even in Lampasas, knew the Herrings. Of course, it wasn't as big a town as it is now.

Everyone loves their pets. So much so that they spend more on their pets than folks did on their own children when I was a kid. It reminds me of a story I heard of a preacher and his pet monkeys. The curious monkeys were playing with an electric wire and were electrocuted. The preacher had heard of taxidermists that 'fixed' animals so they would look alive forever. The preacher took the pair to the taxidermist's shop and asked him to 'fix' them. The man said, "Oh, you want them mounted." This was the common term used. The preacher said, "Oh my Lord, no! Just have them shaking hands or something.!"

Another time when I was probably about three or four years old, Dad was milking the cow and noticed the mare's udder. He had weaned the horse's baby a couple of days previously, and she was in much discomfort. She had a big udder full of milk, and he got this devious idea. He poured the cow's milk out on the ground, and then milked old Blue, the mare. The next night, we had the milk at supper. My sister was gone to a friend's house, the hired hand wouldn't say anything, and Mother had graham crackers in her milk so she couldn't taste it right off. But I complained. Mother said, "That is last night's milk. It's all right. Drink your milk!" A little while later, I said that it tasted salty. Mother said, oh, old Betsy must have eaten a certain kind of weed. She seemed to know it all when it came to food and what I should eat to make me big and tall. (It didn't work!) About the third time I complained, Dad couldn't hold it any longer. He busted out in uncontrollable laughter. Having lived with Dad all those years, Mother got this look on her face and said, "Fred, what is the matter with this milk!" He told her that it was Old Blue's milk, and Mother tossed the rest of her half-drunk glass of mare's milk and graham crackers in his face. This story made the Fort Worth Star Telegram paper.

Once when I was about a year and a half old, we were on our way to a play at school. This was back when small communities used to have women-less weddings and nigger minstrels. These were stage plays done at the school. I was supposed to be a black baby in the play. Of course, I was a little too big for the carriage with my arms and legs hanging over the side of the baby carriage. My parents had colored me black when Dad got another good idea. We were nearly to Jess and Georgie's house when he thought of how they had always wanted to have children and couldn't. Dad cut the headlights on the car and coasted to the gate, then left me at the front door and knocked and hid. When Jess came to the door, you should have heard him scream, "GEORGIE!!"

CHAPTER TWELVE
SEVEN YEAR DROUGHT

Dad and Mother had bought the Seneca, Missouri, 350-acre ranch during the seven-year drought in Texas in the 1950s as many other Texas farm and ranch people had done. The Missouri ranch would have run nearly as many cattle as the Texas ranch would because the valley portion of it would support a cow to every acre. The property included the 80-acres of corn growing on it. There was a big, beautiful barn with a huge hayloft and a big upright concrete silo on each side of the barn. One of my first jobs that summer was to paint that barn red and repair the cattle pens. There was a spring by the house that flowed 1350 gallons per minute the year around. It flowed into a banana-shaped pond with a concrete dam at the end. The dirt dam on the lower side from the spring to the concrete dam at the end pushed the water up against the mountain making it the shape of a banana. It had big white oak, hickory, and cottonwood trees on the wide dirt dam. We put picnic tables under the shade trees, and it was as pretty as any park I have ever seen. We borrowed the neighbor's Percheron workhorse and slip so that the horse could pull and move the sediment out of the bottom of the pond to make it deeper. The workhorse would pull the slip out with a big load of sediment, while our saddle horse would pull the unloaded slip back in. The workhorse pulling one way, and the saddle horse pulling the other way coming back in. It was too muddy for a tractor. When we finished, we shut the floodgates and watched the pond fill up with water.

Dad was a young man then, and he said, "Last one in is a rotten egg!" We stripped to our shorts and dove off the dam. It was so cold we nearly walked on water. When we checked the temperature, it was 57 degrees. He said that this is no swimming pool, so we made a trout pond out of it. The water flowed through the pond so quickly that no vegetation would grow in it, and we had to feed the trout daily like chickens. Dad had always loved to eat fish, but he didn't have the patience to catch them. He said, "Now, I have them where I want them. If I can't catch them, we will drain the water and pick them up off the ground." It wasn't a problem to catch them, though. We had friends visiting from Texas that had a good time catching and grilling the fish outside. Before we moved back to Texas, we did drain the pond and have a fish fry for all the neighbors.

When the corn was at its juiciest stage, we put it up in the silos to ferment and make feed for the cattle for the winter. Dad cut the corn stalks with a horse-drawn Row Binder that had been adapted to pull with a tractor. It cut and tied a seven-foot long bundle about a foot in diameter. Our neighbor brought a wagon and team of horses. He and I pitch forked the bundles onto the wagon and hauled them back to the silos. We pitch forked them one at a time to a grinder powered by a tractor that cut them in two-inch lengths, and blew them through a tube to the tops of the silos until they were full. On the end of a pitchfork, they were very heavy and more so with the leverage of the pitchfork! After doing this all day, every day for days, I was in good condition when football practice started.

Driving a team of horses was a different experience. You could even be on the ground pitching bundles of feed on to the wagon and give commands to the horses. 'Get up' to go and 'Whoa' to stop. 'Gee' to go left and 'Haw' to go right. When I was ten or so years old back in Texas, my friend, Max Kendrick and I would ride horseback several miles to see each other and spend the night. We would start at the same time and meet in the middle, then ride the rest of the way together. There was only a small percent of the cars on the highway, compared to the numbers, today. The Kendricks lived on Highway 183 south of Lometa, so we would show off to people passing by on the road. We trained our horses to kind of bow their heads and turn to the right together as we swept our hats off to them. We got lots of honking of car horns. The Kendricks moved to the Pickett house less than a mile away when we were about twelve, and we had different kinds of experiences with our horses. When it came a big snow, we pulled our sisters on tin sleds roped to the horse's saddles.

We were not fourteen years old yet, so we were too young to get our driver's licenses. I swapped a hog that I had raised from a 4-H project to Uncle Mert Hood for his old gig. A gig is a two-wheeled cart that has a seat for two people, two buggy wheels with a shaft that went on both sides of the horse to just in front of the shoulders. Of course, Dad had the experience and knew how to teach a horse to pull our gig. Max and I could go to town in style, and the girls all wanted a ride.

One day, Max said, "Let's try my little sister's smaller Welsh horse." The mare kept trying to turn too quick inside the shaves on each side instead of making a sweeping, rounding turn. Just like twelve year olds, we figured a solution. If the pony could see the situation, then she could understand what to do. I told Max to go get Red's bridle, and I took the blind bridle off the little mare. She looked back and saw all that mess attached to her, and she took off like a bat out of hell. She hit the windmill with one wheel, broke the gig loose and scattered the harness all over the pasture. We never got it all back together again.

Back in Missouri

Dad would have had to invest a lot of money to make the Missouri ranch reach its full potential, and Mother and Dad had just gotten so homesick and wanted to move back home in Texas. I was sixteen, 165 pounds and tough from the farm work and played first-string fullback on the offense and linebacker on defense for a team that didn't lose a game all year. Sports were big at Seneca, and I made friends pretty quick. It was a school about the size of Lampasas at that time. Also, I boxed in the Golden Gloves at Joplin, Missouri. So I was happy, but Mother grew up on the Ivey ranch, which was just one ranch between it and the Herring ranch, and she was homesick. Dad was born at home with the help of Jess Pickett's black mother, Aunt Silvia.

Even after we moved back to Texas, I visited with my friends in Missouri several times. We wrote letters back and forth to keep in contact. Years later, the Seneca team had been to the State playoffs several times, and the team was going to play the State game again. To get people more enthused about the football game and parade, the players from the first winning team of 1953 were invited to be introduced at the game and ride a parade float.

Our family stayed in Missouri one and a half years, and just couldn't stay away from home any longer. Dad hired semi-trucks to haul our cattle back to Texas and they stayed on to sell the Missouri property, and sent me to take care of the livestock. No pickup, just a couple of horses. My sister was in college. Those three summer months, I stayed with Grandma in the big old colonial two-story house. She did have a twelve-year-old Chevy car that I cleaned up and used on Saturday nights. Like I mentioned before, the screwworm problem kept me busy and with Dad giving me all this responsibility, I wanted to do a good job. With no TV back then, Grandma went to bed with the chickens. As a sixteen year old, I was so bored that sometimes, if there was enough moonlight, I would slip out, saddle Red and ride up the mountain. At night a wind is rare, and it was just indescribably peaceful. I thought that heaven couldn't be much better. I could see the moonlight reflect off of the Santa Fe Lake, lights in Lometa and lights in San Saba twenty miles away. A couple of miles away at the east side of the ranch, I could see an occasional steam engine come by and hear the lonesome whistle at the crossings. The horse would not disturb the night animals and birds, so I had company.

I am not an 'animal rights' person because God said he put them here for our use. My horses have always agreed after they got used to the idea. I have always loved all kinds of animals, and animals have always got along pretty well with me. A dog has never bitten me, even though they may have bitten others. Like with some people, they just naturally like you and will come to you as a friend. I think God, and my forefathers, put me here for a purpose.

CHAPTER THIRTEEN
FIRST SCHOOL RODEO

In the summer of 1953, the Lometa Future Farmers classes had been planning a school rodeo. Their instructor, Thurman Head, had served in the 'Remount' in Burma during WWII. Horses and mules that were supposed to already be broke to ride were shipped to him, and he had to see about training them. Horses and mules were still used in wars at that time because of the very rough terrain. Unlike vehicles, they could go almost anywhere a man could go. Soon the rest of the troops wanted to watch the training. Mr. Head had done a little rodeo himself, and this gave him the idea for us.

Mr. Head and several other local Lometa ranchers had rodeo experience and thought the kids would like it, too. There were no rodeo facilities in Lometa or any of the adjoining towns, so the school football field was converted. Net wire was strung around the outside of the light poles, and pens were wired together with truck and pickup sideboards. A lot of skinned legs came out of these chutes when the bucking stock was turned out. But these were tough country boys. There were no girls in FFA back then and this rodeo was just for Lometa FFA. Later when an arena was built, it was opened up to several joining counties, thus the name Lometa Invitational Youth Rodeo. This was the first youth rodeo, at least that anyone knew of.

The rodeo livestock were donated by many of the local ranchers. Goats were cheaper and easier to handle, so they were used for the roping and calf scramble. Big Brahman cross "past yearlings" were for riding instead of bulls and were actually harder to ride because they hit the ground more times and were so much quicker than bulls. I thought I could stay on anything for eight seconds, but soon as I cleared the chute, I started slipping, or may be it was that loose hide slipping me over to the side. Next, like a cat, that 800-pound yearling caught me in the chest with both hind feet and pulled me loose, and then stepped on me. No one stayed on during that rodeo. The kids practiced before the rodeo at night with the help and advice of the veteran rodeo dads. One night, Berley Hightower asked me to try out his horse, but he failed to mention that the horse didn't like spurs, and I always rode with spurs. All the old timers got a kick out of it when I goosed him, and he went to bucking. Since we didn't have any bucking horses as an event, they said I should do that at the rodeo. So that night when I got down in front of the bleachers, I goosed him, and he really put on a show! I didn't have a flank girt on my saddle, and after a little, the saddle was nearly up on his neck. So, I pulled his head up to stop the bucking, got off and loosened the front girt and slid it back. Someone said, "Oh, he must have a burr under the blanket," They must of thought my show was an accident, then when I got back on, spurred him again, and he went to bucking.

Dad had a horse that a friend had given him that had been raced and was a little crazy. Every time you leaned forward, he would take off like he was running a race and was hell to stop. Dad took him because he was free. He always said, "Don't look a gift horse in the mouth - for his age or anything else." We had a neighbor boy that wanted to borrow the horse for the rodeo, and I told him the horse was crazy. He knew that, but he wanted to win the race, he said. The straight drag race was from goal post to goal post on the football field. When the hat fell, the race was on, and Charles past me and Red # 1 and everyone else and went right on out the gate into the dark hollering WHOA! For a while, all we could hear was the fading WHOA, Whoa, whoa. The crowd loved it! But I felt responsible and was afraid he would get hurt. The horse finally ran down, and he came riding back to get his ribbon. The next year, the rodeo was held in a new and better wire and board facility just below the football field. Ten years later, my FFA classes started building all steel facilities during shop classes and completed them in six years.

CHAPTER FOURTEEN
NATURE- FROM THE BACK OF A HORSE

A cowboy that is out in nature by himself all hours of the day and night sees all the animals and birds. He gets to understand their nature and the habitat they live in. He understands that the individual species have cycles that are controlled by disease, predators and 'their' cycles. At the bottom of the cycles, the animals become hard to find, but after a few years, they are on the increase again. Another experience I had with animals and a different habitat was the summer I went to summer school in Alpine, Texas at Sul Ross University. Uncle Rex and his family took me on a Sunday afternoon drive up to Fort Davis. The mountains on the way were so big and pretty that I commented that I would really like to ride a horse into and camp in those mountains. He said that he had leased one of the big ranches one time and would get permission from the owner so I could do just that. Soon after that, I went home for my sister's wedding and brought back my saddle and camping equipment. A bedroll, army mess kit, two-quart water canteen and a small pot to cook in. It had to be lightweight so most of the food had to have water mixed with it.

Rex drew me a map in the dust on the ground of the huge, single pasture that would take over two days to ride around. He said that he would pull my horse with a trailer and take me out, but when I got to his place, the horse was there, but Rex wasn't. I did not want to wait, so I rode about fifteen miles to the ranch and many more miles to the spring he had told me about. This was the July the Fourth holidays in West Texas, so it was hot and dry. Well, the spring was dry, and so was I and the poor horse! It was about dark by then, and I had to stake the horse and rest 'til morning. I was worried that the horse might not be broke to stake and would run off and leave me. Seemed like Rex couldn't be right about everything. I didn't get much sleep that first night, watching to be sure the horse didn't pull loose from the stake. The grass is so sparse out there that I had to move the staked horse as often as I could every time I stopped for a meal, mornings and evenings.

The next morning we were off to find that windmill. When I found it, the wind wasn't blowing, but there was water in the trough. There was no storage tank; the trough would simply run over when it was full. I hung my canteen under the facet and climbed the mill and turned the wheel by hand. After we were satisfied, we climbed to the top of the mountain to cross and couldn't believe how pretty it was. It was much higher than our mountains back home, windy and I could see for many miles. There were different types of birds and animals, too. The good part of being alone is the quiet, and being able to hear the wind and natural surroundings. There was no livestock, cattle, so it was like I was exploring new uninhabited land., It is just a lot different than being with others. Well, I can't remember the horse's name, we started down to the other side to find that spring creek, but about half way down a canyon, we came to a cliff. We worked our way back to the top again and went down another canyon only to find another cliff. We would work back up to the top and find another canyon to go down and the same thing would happen. I thought I would have to go back to the windmill and go home, but finally I found a canyon where we could make it all the way down to the bottom.

The creek was easy to find and had water. Me and the horse was ready for it, and it looked so inviting that I decided to put my bed-roll on the sand by the creek until I found a rattlesnake enjoying it, too. I had seen deer, all kinds of birds and animals, but no mountain lions. So I decided it would be best for both me and the horse to get away from that creek to make camp. By the time we got out of the pasture and down the highway back to Alpine, the third day, we were both pooped and a sight to see and smell. Rex chided me about the poor old horse. I think he was just joking though. It was quite an experience for a nineteen-year-old boy.

(Back at our ranch) Since Grandma went to bed early, she got up early. And early in the cool of the morning, the animals that were hid in brush or between big rocks with a case of screwworms would be out grazing. That was the best time to find them. Red and I would be out there before the sun was up good. The night animals, like a mother coon and several babies following would be heading back home. We had foxes, possums, rabbits, and squirrels, but no deer back then. At that time of day, the animals were usually out, and being an animal lover, this is why I have always loved to get up early.

When I found a wormy, I would have to drive the animal back to the barns and doctor it. Then re-treat it along with the others when needed. After driving it back, I had to go back and look some more. Sometimes an unruly cow would have to have company to drive it, so I would have to take the others back to the herd. This work, along with repair work on fences, gates and corrals kept me busy. Spanish Oak trees have a short life and seem to blow down on the fences pretty often. Cutting the tree limbs off and repairing the fence on the side of the steep part of the mountain and walk on all those rolling stones was, and still is, a hard chore.

When friends or city relatives would come to visit, we would take off and sit on the porch and drink ice tea. They always would say how nice it would be to do this for a living. They didn't know about all the blood, sweat and tears. Still, I wouldn't swap places with them. More about the blood, later.

CHAPTER FIFTEEN
EVERY DAY LIFE IN THE OLD DAYS

By the end of that summer of 1953, my folks moved back to the little limestone house across the road from Grandma's. At this point, I should mention what life was like living in the country 'before' 1953. There were no electric lines in the rural part of the country, anywhere until about 1948. People used kerosene lamps for light, and wood for fuel to cook and warm their homes. Since there were no chainsaws, they had only an axe to cut wood. They usually cut and stacked a good supply near the house so they wouldn't have to do it during the busy seasons. Winter was a good time to chop wood because a person got pretty hot doing that chore. They had to keep a good supply because they didn't know when they might be too sick or wet and stormy weather to do it. Some parts of the world used whale or seal oil, but most used hog fat to cook with. People had to make their own salad dressing and other flavoring foods. The hogs were bred for fat more than meat. The process to make vegetable cooking oil had not come of age.

Our house had a kitchen with a wood cook stove, a living room with a fireplace, and two bedrooms with a small bath between them. A wood heater in the master bedroom heated the bath and the smaller bedroom, slightly. Fire wood was stacked just out side a window, so it was quick and easy to get another log for the fire. Years later, when dad build a new house, he had a false cabinet built beside the fire place that he could stack wood from his pickup right into the wood box. Then open the doors from inside the house to get the wood.   Water for baths was heated in kettles on the bed-room heater. It didn't take much water or long to take a bath on a cold winter night.

When my sister and I were very small, we slept on bunk beds in Mother and Dad's room. She was on the top one, and since I was two and a half years younger, I was on the bottom. We couldn't afford much luxury, but since Dad didn't drink he thought he could afford a not-so-expensive King Edward cigar. He took great pleas-ure in cutting the end off, licking it and lighting it. He noticed his little two-year-old son watching every move, and he asked me if I would like to smoke it. Of course! Mother had a wild-eyed fit, but Dad assured her that he knew what he was doing. (Going to break me of the habit at a very young age.) She said, you will clean up the mess! Well, it didn't happen until the lights were out when I started complaining and throwing up. Mother kicked Dad and said OK. He was in his usual nighttime apparel, shorts, with a pan and a wet rag when my sister looked off the top bunk just over us. It didn't take as long for her to get sick as it did me. She threw up right on Dad's bare back and shoulders with it running down under his neck, too. "Ruth! Look what these kids have done to me!"

When my sister, Mary Kay, was old enough, Dad said she could have the guest room all to herself. Not very long afterwards, he built a prefab room for me outside the main house, about three feet from it. He had ordered this small building to store grain, but it got there too late to use for the grain. So he got a friend to help him put it up and cut windows and a door. It was an all-board floor and walls bolted together without a lot of trim, except for the pretty green grass that grew up between the walls and floor. He said I could do anything I wanted, but I had to live in it. My favorite thing was shooting wasps with my BB gun. I had to throw the covers over my head to keep from getting hit by a ricochet BB. I was quite a bit older before my all-knowing older cousins told me why Mother and Dad wanted me out of their bedroom. Some years after that, one of our dove hunters that owned several movie theaters gave me a twelve by ten glossy picture of Marylene Monroe. I had exchanged pictures in the frame on my dresser, when Dad came in and said, "I wondered when old Red was going to be replaced."

For country people, we were 'up town' because we had an indoor bathroom. I know because I visited friends that had toliets outside. The businesses in Lometa had theirs out in the back alley. There were no electric appliances, so if you couldn't do it with kerosene or wood, you did it by hand. When we went outside, we carried kerosene lanterns instead of flashlights and heated solid steel irons on the wood cook stove to iron clothes. There was a room at the end of our car garage, separate from the house, for clothes washing.

Everyone put their garage away from the house when automobiles first became popular. Monday was washday for Mother, and Dad would get the fire going under the big tub of water before going to work. Mother always put on a pot of pinto beans because they didn't have to be watched while she was out washing. We knew what was for dinner on Mondays! Unlike many, we had a modern gasoline powered washing machine, but the wringer to squeeze the water out of the clothes was a hand-cranked unit. And, of coarse, then it was to the cloths lines.

The only batteries I remember were a six-volt car battery that powered the radio and a smaller battery to power the telephone.

The telephone lines for each farmer or rancher had to be erected and maintained through his property by the owner. It was tied into the neighbors, and each had his own number of rings to identify who was to pick up the party line phone. The main problem with the system was the old gossips on the line. The system was owned by everyone, and they paid a lady in town, Lometa, to be the switchboard operator. If you called someone that was not on your line, you called the operator with one ring and told her to get so and so. Her name was Happy. Happy loved her job and was so accommodating that she could tell you where the person could be found if she wasn't at home and when she was expected to return. For the young people, she was a pretty good dating service. When I would come in from college, Texas A&M was an all-male military school, I would ask Happy to get Fay on the line. Happy would say that she already has a date. Then get Maxine. She left with some girls. Then I would ask, "Happy, who is available?" And she would set me up with a date for Saturday night.

Since there were no deep freeze appliances, some rural neighbors had a meat club. Approximately twelve would supply a calf a month, so that they would have fresh beef some times every month of the year. These were usually a milk cow's calf that was 'milk fat' and out of a Jersey cow and a Hereford bull. Nothing like a feedlot beef like everyone is used to eating today. They just don't have the same taste, but if that is all you have ever had, you don't know what you are missing. Just like animals raised in confinement today, compared to the ones raised on free range. They don't know what they are missing and are as happy as can be. So what is the big fuss?

Everyone had egg-laying hens and 'eating chickens', by the way, they ran free, too. When you had unexpected company, just go out and catch a chicken. Don't get any fresher than that! People thought nothing of pulling the head off so they would bleed out, plucking the feathers and gutting the chicken. Today the average housewife would throw up if she had to do that, and would not even know how to cut up a dressed chicken. Mother ran around two hundred laying hens and sold eggs at the same place in Lometa that she bought the protein feed for the chickens. We raised the grain. When she went to pick out the sacks that the feed came in, it took a while, because the feed companies put the feed in sacks made of cotton material that the house wife could use to make clothes. It took so many sacks of one print to make a dress for herself and not so much for me a shirt. She wasn't particular for dad's shorts, because no one would see them, but us. Sometimes she would just use a cattle salt sack. I remember my sister seeing Dad in his shorts, and saying, "Daddy, you have a windmill on your tee hindee." The Great Depression days were hard, but ranch people still had a good time.

Each family raised a few hogs and butchered on a cold day, so the meat wouldn't spoil before they got it processed, then smoked and cured the meat and let it hang in the smoke house. It would be good, wouldn't spoil, and be available for a long time. The lard was processed for cooking oil; cracklins was a by-product of that. Lye soap was usually made at this time. Most everyone in the country did this. Many years later when they would visit someone with their house air conditioned and set pretty cold, the country visitor would say "it's cold enough to kill hogs"

Springtime was when people plowed and planted the garden. Then as the different vegetables and fruits ripened through the summer, they were canned or put in jars for the rest of the year. This canning was done through a heating process that took the air out to make it last. The date was put on the lids so the old would not get mixed with the current jars. It took a lot of sugar to put up fruit. During the World War II, sugar was rationed so that we didn't get to put up much fruit. We were very careful not to waste it. Once when I had boys visiting me and one was dumping several spoons full of sugar into his ice tea, Dad said "stir like hell, we don't mind the noise." We even made a trip to Old Mexico to buy sugar, and other things that were hard to get in Texas.

The most problems people had with rationing was the shortage of gasoline and tires. You had to have stamps, as well as money, to buy gasoline, and when you ran out, you walked. Kind of like you do in most other countries now. Walk. They ride a lot of bicycles or little motorbikes. When you couldn't get new tires, you ran those 'old rags' until they just wouldn't hold air any longer. Many people fixed their own flats because when the tires were that thin, they got a lot of flats. Also, tires were reinforced with natural fibers which were nowhere near as strong as the synthetic ones we have today

Back then, there was no government aid. Period! Churches and good people helped the needy, and cities had soup lines that people stood in line to get something to eat. People in the cities could raise none of the food that the country people had and many were actually malnourished. I hope it never gets that bad again, but my parent's generation have been watching for it ever since. What would it be like if we couldn't get petroleum? Tractors couldn't run, trucks couldn't deliver food and goods to the cities. Little things that are synthetic like clothes, those tires we talked about and half of the other stuff you own has something that comes from oil. We would have to go back to the horses, and hog lard to cook with. Thank the Lord, we have enough oil and gas here in the USA to last for generations, if the so-called Environmentalists will let us use it before we get to that point.

CHAPTER SIXTEEN
SHEEP AND GOATS

Sheep are so slow and dumb that they are nearly impossible to drive without a good dog. They will just stand there and do nothing. If they lay with their feet uphill, they can't get back up. One hot summer day, Dad noticed sheep coming to the water trough by the barn. A little later, he noticed they were still coming and going. They travel in the heat of the day single file with their head in the shade of the rear end of the one in front of them. The first one to the water trough had a drink and some way stuck her head under the last one, and they were just traveling in a circle. Several hundred sheep! Dad had to go out and kick one out of line to break the circle and start a new line. This is called milling. Some people are so dumb that they will follow other people doing the wrong thing. Maybe that is why in the Bible, Jesus talks about leading His Sheep.

Goats are much different. When you are moving goats, they will run to the edge of the mountain where you can't see the ones in the front of the flock turn back and run away in the brush to the side of the mountain, or the goats will split up. If you catch a sheep, she won't say a thing, but the goat will scream bloody murder!

Dad sold all of his Angora goats to a neighbor just across the fence from us on the other side of the mountain. The goats kept coming back, and I had gone over that fence with a fine-toothed comb! They say if you can throw water through a fence, a goat can get through it. We took the goats back again, and I took some water and food with me and waited and waited and watched until they got to the fence. They had found a big rock on the neighbor's side of the fence. One at a time, the goats hopped up on the rock and jumped over the five-foot fence.

In that big rough brushy mountain pasture, we had missed a few goats. They multiplied so fast we soon had a bunch more, since they may have twins twice a year. We thought we got them all up and sold them. But soon we saw some babies that had grown up. Dad swore saying, "Looks like we never will be able to get rid of all those dam things."

Seems like sheep are always looking for a place to die, but sometimes the Angora goats were nearly as bad. They eat brush and very little grass. So we would find them with their long curly white hair hung up in brush or briars where they couldn't get out. Angora goats don't have as much meat and muscle as other types of goats, so that hair would get weighed down with mud and water when they went to get a drink from a dirt tank or a pond. The water had gotten so low, and the goats would get stuck in the mud. In the hot summer sun, they would die if you didn't find them soon. This was another thing that the horseback cowboy had to watch for. Pitch his rope over their heads and drag them out. I have even found goats hanging from a limb. The goat had reared up on his hind feet to pull a limb down, from a tree, where he could eat the leaves, and got his foot hung in a fork of a limb. The limb will spring back up either leaving the goats' hind feet in the air or barely touching the ground. Sometimes we found them too late.

We would shear the sheep and goats in the spring, and the goats again in the fall. That was always a big day or two getting the number of men that was needed to shear the size of flock that we had at that time. They brought all their equipment, and a kid or a girl, to gather the wool off the shearing floor and put it on a table. We provided the table and strings to tie each fleece of wool (Goat hair didn't have to be tied) and the person to tie it. Usually, Dad or I would do this job because the fleece could be cleaned up and the shorter wool tucked inside, which could make it appear better and sell for a better price. Eight-foot sacks with two racks to hold them open were by the table, and a person in the sack to catch the fleece when it was tossed to them. They placed the best side out, inside the sack then tamped it down. Small cuts on the animals, if any, were doctored and a paint brand was placed on the left hip. When we had screwworms, we kept those sheared sheep or goats in a small trap pasture for a week or so to make sure they didn't get a case of screwworms. Since the shearing day was so labor intensive, neighbors helped each other similar to the grain thrashing days.

CHAPTER SEVENTEEN
FARMING

Grandpa raised grains and row crops like corn and cotton. It took a lot of mules and horses to farm the Herring and Pickett 450 acres of cropland because it was so much slower than with machinery. This was a big farm and ranch in its day since the average size was about 350 acres with only a small amount of the land in cultivation. Our ranch was 1,800 acres total including the cropland. The cropland had to be broke, disked, planted and harvested—with mules and horses! In the early days of thrashing, the grain was cut with a horse-drawn mower. A buck rake pushed it to the thrasher where it was put into the thrasher with pitchforks. In later years, the row binder cut the crops and put it in bundles that were pitch forked to the horse-drawn wagon and taken to and forked to the thrasher. The thrasher was a huge machine powered by steam.

Grandpa told of one time the thrasher came before they had planned, and grandpa didn't have the wood cut. It took a lot of wood to power the machine for days of thrashing and he was upset, saying he didn't know how he could do everything necessary to get ready and cut wood, too. Neighbor Jess Pickett told him that it would be cut and delivered by morning. He cut wood all night, with an axe, and hauled the wood to the field by early morning.

The big machine was located so the grain would not have to be hauled further than necessary. It thrashed the grains from the stalks. From there it was sacked and hauled to the grain bins inside the barns. The stacks of straw would get so big that occasionally the machine would have to be moved. The straw was left for the cattle when it was needed in the winter when grass was not very plentiful. Later, Grandpa bought his own machine since he had so much grain, and built a tall barn especially for the thrasher machine. It was quite an investment, and he wanted to take care of it.

The barn is still standing today. It took a lot of men to do all of this work at harvesting time and a lot of fuel to run them, so neighboring women helped the resident housewife on this job, too. Remember, there was no electricity and only wood cook stoves. Since it was hot summer time, it was just as hot in the kitchen as in the fields. There was an old saying: "Eating like a thrashing crew."

The fields that had corn and/or cotton had to be cultivated at least twice to keep the weeds from taking over. This did not have to be done with the grain because the rows of grain were closer together and shaded the ground so the weeds didn't come up. Both the corn and cotton had to be harvested by hand. Every plant! About 1945, Dad quit growing the corn and cotton instead of buying a different type of harvesting machine for it. He couldn't compete without it, and he was tired of all the extra work to raise it. He put every field in grain, oats or wheat that could be harvested with a combine pulled by a tractor. It eliminated the two trips across the fields plowing and hoeing weeds. Plus, if conditions were favorable, he could run livestock on it in the winter until March. He had to take the cattle off by March if he planned on harvesting the grain seeds.

I wasn't old enough to remember all of this, but I do remember the first tractor and combine. By the time I was big enough to drag a sack of grain, I rode on the combine, collecting grain in the sacks, sewed them at the top and kicked them off a slide on the side. When the grain was good, it was hard to keep up. Dad drove the tractor that pulled and powered the combine. My job was the worst because of all the dust and chaff. If there was no sign of rain, the sacks of grain could be picked up and hauled later with a pickup truck. These sacks were hauled to the barns and dumped into the bins the same way as with the thrashing machines, minus the horses.

There were three barns spread a ways apart so if one barn ever caught fire, the other barns would not. This was Grandpa's insurance. The barns were built so a team of horses could drive all the way through them with bins on each side. A horse-drawn wagon was hard to back up, and everyone was in a hurry on thrashing day.

CHAPTER EIGHTEEN
KIDS TO COLLEGE

When I was big enough to really make a hand, I worked all summer and after school. Dad didn't believe in allowances, but let me have an FFA or 4-H project, which was a show sheep to begin with. Sears, the catalog people, had a program to let kids have female sheep for free with the understanding that the first female lamb that was born went to another kid. When I was nine years old, I chose Southdowns because they were small, and I could handle them. Later, my dad let me get a show steer. When I was in the tenth grade, I put all my savings into commercial steers and was lucky to sell them at the peak of the price cycle. At that time, I didn't buy back because we were moving to Missouri. This was luck too, because the cycle nosed down. One of the worst cattle busts occurred soon after I sold the calves. So when we got back to Texas my senior year, the prices were real cheap. I wanted to buy some of those cheap cows and start a herd. Dad told me he couldn't afford to let me because times were still hard, and I might put him out of business. Finally, we agreed on a deal where I put all my profit into my college education and worked for him all the summers but one. The numbers of cows in the USA were at an all time high, which made them cheap. I was able to buy fourteen top quality Hereford heavy bred heifers for $85 each with the money I had saved from the good years. They all delivered healthy calves within a month or so after I bought them. After a couple of years, the prices gradually started up. That was the deal of my life.

Those cows sent me through Texas A&M at $900 per year. It was a military college and that price included uniforms, laundry, room and board, and tuition. There were no girls at Texas A&M, and Dad wouldn't let me have a car, even though I had a Model A Ford in part of my high schools days. So, it didn't take much more than the $900 per year. Back then, boys could entertain themselves without spending a lot of money. Like water fights, Comet cleaner bombs, 'stack the room', put skunks in the Air Force dorm. We even put a boy's little Austin-Healy car in the hall of the dorm one night. The next morning when he opened the door of his room, there was his car in the hall.

After I was gone to college, Grandma missed my daily visits, so she sent a lot of letters. Her mind was sharp for an 88 year old, and she kept up with current events, even of my friends. Of course, she missed Grandpa. She got sick, and Mother called me to come home because she was asking for me. Grandma was pretty bad off when I got home, and she sent everyone else out of the room. We had a good long talk of past and future. She said she knew I loved the ranch as much as Dad and Grandpa, and hoped I could keep it together. I swore on her deathbed I would. Being raised around animals through their short life spans, I understood death. I knew

she was going to be with God and Grandpa. And people like Will
Rogers. They idolized Will Rogers; and thought the world of him.

As soon as I graduated from college, I had to go to the Army.
After I got out, I sold the original 14 cows at over twice what I gave
for them. I bought a brand new 1959 Chevrolet with just a little
over what I had received for the cows. Fourteen cows wouldn't buy
much of a car today. Being young and single, it looked like the best
thing to do at the time. With a college education, I should be able
to make lots of money. How many others thought the same thing?
After working three years for the Agriculture Extension Service at
Coleman, I saw that I sure wasn't going to buy a ranch on that salary. I did find and marry Mary Ann Crowder. I just never could
remember people's birthdays, and hers was the day before mine-so
she was the logical one. We decided to move back to the ranch
and live in a little rent house on the west end of the ranch that my
Dad's sister owned.

CHAPTER NINETEEN
HABITAT AND CYCLES

Ten years of teaching Vocational Agriculture to Future Farmers of America, FFA, and a financial note for half interest on equipment and a few cows helped me get started.

The largest half of the Herring ranch is on the mountain and the north side is in rocky brushy pastures totaling about 1,000 acres. Since there are so many rocks on top of the ground and under it, there isn't much deep soil to grow grasses for cattle, but it is good habitat for goats the year round. Lots of rocks to play on and brush to eat.

The hot summer sun dries the ground out pretty fast, so we use it for winter grazing for the cattle. Many years ago, it had a lot of short oak brush that we call shinery. This was excellent for the goats, because like deer, they don't eat grass. They may appear to, but what they are eating is forbs. One form or another grows the year around down close to the ground between the grasses. Back then, the wool and mohair from sheep and goats was a good price because synthetics had not been invented and dad and Grandpa had always had a lot of sheep and Angora goats. Goats have babies twice a year if they are in good condition, and some have twins. There were enough old timers that liked to hunt with their hound dogs, and they kept the coyotes and big red foxes thinned out enough that we could raise these pretty curly-haired white babies. They were called 'kids' because they cried like human kids.

After the hound dog men died, the predators increased to a point that ranchers could not raise babies - sheep or goats. At first it was just cutting into the profits, then later, there would be none to survive. All ranchers carry a gun in their pickup truck to protect their flock from predators. Like Jesus mentioned, "Thy rod and Thy staff." The gun is an important tool for ranchers. We can't be with the animals twenty-four hours a day, so we put bells on a small percent of them. The ringing bells will warn us if the animals are being chased. Before central air and heat, people left a window partially open at night and since there usually isn't any wind at night, we could hear the bells from a great distance. Nighttime, close to day light was usually the time that animals were attacked. Many times, if they were close enough to hear or the wind was right, we grabbed the 30-30 and 12 gauge pump shot gun loaded with buck shot and raced to the rescue.

Sometimes it would be a pack of town dogs. Once, we had one get away, and since we knew he was headed for town, we got back on the county road and found him just inside the city limits. We recognized the dog, and knew it was the same one because he was so tired from being chased. It was just getting to be good light when we caught up with him. Dad was driving and told me to shoot. I leaned out the truck window with the pump shotgun and blew him right off the road right there in town. In nature, there is a law of survival of the fittest, and we humans are the fittest because of our God given intelligence. Of course, there are some that don't have it. Dad always believed in quick, sure punishment. This may sound harsh, but once a dog or most any animal kills, he will be a killer for life. All ranch people realize this and understand what has to be done, even if it is one of their own good sheep dogs. We had to kill one of our good Border collie sheep dogs. The Bible talks about capital punishment for humans, too.

After people lost so much money on their goats and sheep, they stopped raising them. Then here came another predator or invader, the cedar trees. If cedar is allowed to spread and cover the ground, grass will not grow under it because it shades the sun all twelve months of the year. You have to continue the fight because you never get rid of the cedar. The cedar has devastated the land. Cedar is called an invader because it is not native to this country. The grass holds the soil together, where the cedar doesn't and the soil is washed away to the Gulf of Mexico. When a raindrop hits on grass, the speed of the raindrop is cushioned and the water goes down the stems and roots of the grass and into the underground water supply, the aquifer. But not so with the cedar. Because of another invader, not native to this country, the animal rights people thought the little Golden Cheek Warbler could not survive unless we left all these cedars alone.

CHAPTER TWENTY
RANCHERS- INDEPENDENT PEOPLE

In 1994, President Clinton and Texas Governor Ann Richards forwarded legislation that would ruin a big part of our state and its water capturing ability by stopping the cutting and removal of cedar. Ranch people are not easily run over, as shown in the "Abilene Reporter-News article from July 22, 1994:"

Ranchers ready to 'kill' for land rights by J. T. Smith, Farm Editor

"Voluntary programs work. Government mandates don't.

Top USDA officials heard this message over and over from farmers and ranchers who came to Abilene from throughout Texas Thursday for the Natural Resource Conservation Forum.

The forum welcomed thousands of words of testimony from six panels and dozens of speakers – including statements from two open microphone sessions.

Rancher Travis Herring gave the listening panel a strong message to take back to Washington. Herring operates a 2,000-acre ranch near Goldthwaite that has been in his family since 1889. But without the control of cedar, it would just be worthless brush, he noted. But, controlling cedar lets grasses flourish and allows water to recharge the underground aquifer. The seasoned rancher noted that if his area is declared a 'critical habitat' for the golden cheek warbler, he might as well quit ranching. Herring says if he and other ranchers are prohibited from controlling the cedar, it would amount to the same as taking their ranches away from them. Taken by cedar brush, his land would be rendered useless.

The U. S. Fish and Wildlife Service has proposed 33 Texas counties as 'critical habitats' for the warbler. Such designation would grab 20.5 million acres of Texas land, including three Big Country counties of Stephens, Palo Pinto and Erath.

Herring hopes a showdown never comes. But he and other ranchers will not give up their land, he noted.

"We've sweated and bled over every square foot of it for three generations," Herring said.

Herring noted that he is prepared to die for his family ranch – if it ever comes to that.

"And I would kill for it," Herring assured.

His fellow ranchers also are "up in arms" over the proposed intrusion into their private property, he reported.

(The Washington panel had looked like they were asleep and unconcerned with all the other participates up until this point. I wanted them to wake up and see our determination. So, I stopped talking and just stood there waiting for their response)

At the end of the warning, the moderator asked if other ranchers felt this strongly. He told him that weekend and retired city people living in the country might not, but those like me that are married to the land, will!" (Also, a couple of weeks later they marched on Austin and stopped the proposed legislation.)

CHAPTER TWENTY-ONE
REX IVEY - BIG BEND RANCHER

At this point, maybe I should inject a little information about the Ivey genetics of this generation of Herrings. Rex 'Papa' Ivey was of Irish decent and passed his short fuse characteristic on to his three boys and two daughters. Rex Ivey first drove for Wells Fargo, the stagecoach route between San Angelo and Sonora, Texas. This was one of the sparsely populated areas of West Texas of which many books have been written. I am sorry to say that I didn't get much information from him about it. Only that it was a long, lonely trip. He told a little of the problems with the mules and the wheels of the wagons carrying the heavy loads. Papa Ivey was younger than Grandpa and not crippled in his legs like Grandpa.

When he and Mama Ivey were about seventy years old, they bought a house in town and moved from the ranch. Papa kept his cows and goats and went to the ranch every day. The big ranch house was rented, so he built a tiny little house at the other end of the ranch.. It had a fireplace so he could build a fire, and prop his feet up while he had his lunch. Then, he took a nap after lunch, or dinner as they called it. One day he came in from the ranch all skinned up. Mother and her sister, Mary Ethel McAnelly, that ran a dry goods store in Lometa, really got on to him for being too reckless at his age. He had driven up to his cabin for lunch and saw a goat run out from under a shed heading for the brushy mountain. He grabbed his old horse and didn't take time to put a saddle on him and was going to head him off before he got there. He said he just knew that goat had screwworms. Papa told his daughters that when the horse caught up with the goat, the goat did a quick right turn and so did his horse, without the saddle, "I didn't." He was 75 at the time.

Mama Ivey had long red hair done up on top of the head like most women of the day. And she was of Irish decent, too. Most of my life, working with my dad on the ranch when I would lose my temper with the livestock, he would say, "Now, that's the Ivey blood cropping out." Working with livestock, you have lots of opportunities to lose your temper.

Rex Ivey II had a very interesting life, so we'll use him as an example of our genetics. Life was too dull around Lometa and crowding him a little, so at age sixteen, he went as far due west as he could to the Rio Grande River near Lajitas and Terlingua. He trapped, sold furs, and wax weed to get started ranching. His first thirteen sections were around Lajitas where he lived. Later he married and had two boys, but they lived in Alpine. Lajitas seemed to be the end of the world to his wife because it was a hundred miles to town. The last forty miles to Lajitas was a dirt road, and the last fifteen or twenty miles was no road -- just a dry creek bed that rarely carried water from the mountains. Before he died, he was operating 156 sections, the 100 sections part that was a partnership, and later he and is son Bill bought the old ghost town of Terlingua.

Following are a few stories that reflect the Ivey characteristics.

I was visiting with Bill Wittenburg one day, and he was telling me about his life time old friend, Rex. They were both in their 80s at the time he was telling the story. Bill was on Rex's ranch back in the 1930s deer hunting and couldn't find one, so they rode across the Rio Grande into Old Mexico, seemed like for hours. It was dark when they got back on horseback. He said it was really rough country. Everything had thorns and if it hadn't been for chaps, tough clothes and Taperidoes (leather over the stirrups), they couldn't have stood it.

Rex told him of a friend that was like himself that wanted to go into Mexico to buy cheap cattle and make a little money by re-selling them in Texas. Rex always dressed good and rode a good horse with a pretty fancy saddle and he figured the friend did, too. After traveling several days into Mexico, a couple of Mexicans approached them and visited awhile. Rex could speak Spanish as well as he could English. The Mexicans asked what they would sell their horses and saddles for. Well, Rex couldn't say six words without adding a curse word as an adjective, so he told me I could imagine what he told them. They continued on and bought a pretty good bunch of cattle and started driving them back, when the same two guys and several others approached them again, this time demanding their horses and everything else. Rex and his friend shot one man apiece and got away on their horses and saddles, but no cattle. Bill said he figured he was always watching for the relatives of the dead (if they were) because he always kept a lot of guns around in his car and a pistol under his bedroll at the hunting camps.

Front row: sister Mary Kay, Travis, Mama Ivey, two unknown cowboys. Back row: Fred Herring, Bill Wittenburg, Rex Ivey 2nd, unknown.)

In 1950 my cousin Merlin McAnelly and I went to Lajitas in his WWII jeep to spent a week with Rex on the river place. Going only forty five miles an hour in that old jeep, it took a long time. But I was prepared. Took my Dad's old 22 rifle, and when we got the other side of San Angelo, we rarely saw a car and when we did, we could see it miles away before we met. So, I entertained my self hanging out the side of the jeep shooting beer cans.

There were very few white men within a hundred miles of Lajitas back then. There was just one family living at Terlingua, and one at Lajitus and none between. Besides the store, there was only Rex's house, the farmer's house, and the crumbling ruins of an old fort. There was a small community across the river, but I don't think they had a store because they came to Rex's store for all their supplies. They didn't have an airplane flying the river then. They had the river riders. Every fifteen miles or so, there was a shack and two border patrolmen. One rode horseback in one direction each day watching for livestock or people crossing the river, and the other rode in the opposite direction. They were the Real McCoys, as we used to say. Looked like they were right out of the movies. They were tough; darkly sun tanned young men with high-topped boots, a big hat and pistol with cartridge belt worn low around the waist. Like the native Mexicans, they were riding the Dun Spanish horses that were suited to the tough country. It was tough because of the extreme heat and nearly all of the vegetation had thorns, and, of the people they had to deal with. The border riders would stop by the store for a cool beer, and as boys who grew up watching Roy Rogers and Gene Autry, we got a kick out of visiting with them. They had some pretty good stories, too.

In 1956, I went to summer school at Sul Ross University at Alpine, Texas and visited with the Iveys a lot. I went to Lajitus with uncle Rex about every other weekend. Several times I got Rex's farmer to telling me stories about my uncle. He said that Rex was really hard to work for. Like when one shop worker was hiding from him for something and when Rex found him, the worker started running for the river. Rex jumped in his car and ran him through the trees and nearly caught him, but the worker dove in the river just in time. He said he was sure afraid Rex would have run over him if he had caught up with him.

My boys must have got their love for fast cars from Rex. He never drove a pickup. Said they wouldn't go fast enough. He used to buy two new cars every year and wear them both out. He drove the hundred miles to town as fast as it would go on the straight Big Bend road to Alpine. One day, I was getting my car serviced at the GM dealer and said, "I guess you know my Uncle Rex." The guy said, "Rex is the best advertisement that we have. If he wanted to go to the top of that mountain," he pointed to one, "He would drive as far as he could, then walk the rest of the way." The cars back then didn't have motors that would hold up to continual high speeds as they do today, but the bodies and chassis were stronger. The farmer told of one time it rained on the dirt road between the park road and the river, and the mud packed up in the fender until the front wheels wouldn't turn. That was when the fenders stuck out away from the body of the cars. So, Rex got out his axe and chopped the fenders off the new car and went on his merry way.

In 1960, fellow young County Agriculture Agents, Harry Burleson and Bob Sims, and I were on the Big Bend Park highway on our way to Rex's ranch.

I said to watch for Rex. They asked how will we know him. I told them that he would be the fastest thing that we had seen since we left Lometa. Sure enough, he passed us like we were standing still. And he was pulling a 14-foot trailer behind his Suburban with a jackass in the trailer. I don't know how he lived to a ripe old age. His friends thought he would be shot or killed in a car wreck.

The local newspaper quoted him often and frequently ran his predictions of what kind of winter or spring that they would have. He used signs of nature that the Indians and Mexicans had passed on to him. His oldest son, Rex III, did die before him in a helicopter accident trying to round up some antelope. To date, his younger son, Bill, is still going.

On the hunting trip, Bob, Harry, and I had put our bedrolls at the base of a cliff in a sandy dry creek bed right next to the cliff. Bob had killed a doe for camp meat and hung it from the cliff wall where nothing could get to it. We lay there in our bedrolls under the stars after the fire went out, talking about the wild country we were in.

I told them the Ivey ranch joined the Big Bend Park on its north side, and Rex could not raise baby animals of any kind because of the mountain lions and bears from the Park. After we all went to sleep, something hit me in the ribs and I jumped out of my blankets and hollered! I said that what ever it was, it had claws. When they woke up, they were laughing at me. Bob said, "You were trying to scare us with your stories of lions and scared yourself with a bad dream." I had been lying with my arms in front and my side exposed, and I told them something hit me hard in the side. After laughing at me until they were satisfied, we all turned off the flashlights and lay down, again. There was no moon, just the starlight. Wow!! Right over us there was a pair of green eyes looking down at us from the top of the cliff. All of us grabbed a gun and a flashlight, but after searching for a long time, we couldn't find anything. It took a while then before we could sleep again. I was sleeping very light with my .22 magnum pistol under my pillow. Sometime later in the night, I was aware of a slight noise above me, like something scratching. This time, I eased out my pistol and flashlight and aimed both at the sound before turning the light on. When I did, this furry animal on the cliff above jumped to the ground as I emptied my pistol. I screamed, "I got him!" It was a big coon that had been after that deer ham hanging on the cliff above our bedrolls. So the rejection of my claim that I was not dreaming was vindicated.

Another time, these same two friends and I were hunting mule deer on the government parklands above Pogosa Springs, Colorado. We were scouting canyons on either side of the Continental Divide, mostly looking up. There were more mountain sheep than deer, but we only had permits to shoot one deer a piece. Every once in a while, we would hear rocks falling above us. When we looked in that area, we would see the mountain sheep. The sheep are supposed to be nimble-footed animals; why are they stumbling around in the rocks. We commented that the sheep sure were clumsy, but soon learned the truth. The sheep would back up to a moderate sized rock and use their hind feet to push the rock over the side of the mountain. Harry said, "Those stinking sheep are trying to get rid of us!"

The three of us hunted for free five years on Uncle Rex's ranch. He made most of his living from hunting leases, but he let us young guys hunt this area free because it was such a steep and rough mountain. He said that his high dollar city customers didn't want to work that hard. It was called the 'Rios' river place. We went back to the same place five years in a row and climbed to the top of the mountain as soon as we got there. At that high elevation, it rained more often and caused the grass to grow better. That was the reason the deer were up there. We found a shallow cave near the top that we used so we would not have to pack a tent. The picture on the cover of this book was the front of the cave that we slept in the last several hunts. Note the coffee pot, rifle in back ground and me telling them a story about Rex and the Big Bend. The last year, I only took my 44 Magnum open sights pistol to hunt the mule deer. I had killed white tail with it in the hill country, but wanted to try it there. It would be a long shot in that kind of terrain, but it was my goal and I spent a lot of time in preparation. Got one, too! Bob and Harry came to love that big country as much as I did. There was a US geographical marker, we discovered, that showed the elevation which looked to be near as high as the ones in the Park. From that vantage point, we could see the Rio Grand River and over into Old Mexico, as well as the Park. We did spend time with our scopes looking at the countryside and villages over in Mexico. At this time, we were each in our 20s and felt like we were sitting on top of the world.

Years later, I sold and delivered some cattle to a fellow that had just bought a ranch just north of Lampasas by the name of Lewis R. Tyra. Visiting, after unloading the cattle, I found out his father, Lewis O. Tyra and Walter Mishner were the ones that had bought Lajitus and the land around it from Rex. Walter was big in road construction business and Lewis in the development business in the Houston area. They built a regular old Western town with a motel that looked like a calvery post, board sidewalks, and false front buildings. Several movies have been filmed there, since. Son, Lewis R. said the first time he met Rex, was when his dad sent him to locate the boundries of land they had bought before they bought Lajitus. Rex was to meet him at a certain gate to show him were to start. Lewis, said when he got there, there was a man (Rex) stopped in the road shooting a big deer gun at something down in the bottom of a deep, steep canyon. He looked and there was a man hiding behind a rock yelling for Rex to stop. Rex shot again and cussed him, and the man pleaded with Rex saying to quit "you might hit me." Lewis ask him what was going on. Rex said "I told the blank-ity blank to shoot the deer up here, not down there" Now, we have to carry that thing all the way up to the road. Lewis said that he was a young man then and told him to stop shooting and I will help you carry the deer.! When they got to the bottom of the canyon, the man and Rex laughed and went on like nothing had happened.

An other time, they were in Rex's old looking car, it just looked old, buncing over the pasture roads on a cold day. Son Lewis said that he was freezing and Rex ask if he would like to have some coffee. "Of coarse, said Lewis". The car had over sized mud tires, the back seat gone with a box to sit on and lots of tools and junk back there. Rex stopped and started rummaging around until he found a can of coffee. He took a dip of the coffee, like it was snuff, and handed it to young Lewis.

Later, Lewis, his dad and Rex were hunting mule deer near the Big Bend Park when two Park Rangers drove up and told them that they were hunting on parkland! Rex, with his usual language, told him that he had just sold this land, and he knew where the boundaries were. The ranger told them that he was taking them in. Rex said," No, you aren't!" One ranger pulled his pistol and said, "Yes, I am." Rex raised the muzzle of his big deer rifle and said, "Wonder which one will make the biggest hole? Your little peashooter, or this 30-06? The young fellows got in their vehicle and left without another word. The next day, Rex called the Ranger chief and told him that he didn't want them coming through his property any more. They had been coming through Rex's to get to a part of the park that they could not access with out it. The young rangers didn't know of the agreement.

Mr. Tara had also heard of the time Rex was stopped by a new deputy as he was coming from Alpine. (The deputy must have had a fast car.) Rex asked him if he knew who he was. The deputy said, "Yes, your license says Rex Ivey." Rex said, "Are you still going to give me a ticket?" He did, and Rex told him he would be sorry. Everyone west of the Pecos knew of Rex Ivey, except this new deputy. When Rex got back to the Lajitas store, he told the storekeeper not to sell the deputy any gasoline. Back then, there was no telephone down there nor radios that would reach the hundred miles to Alpine. The deputy didn't have enough gas to get him back, so he had to spend the night in his car. The next day, he caught a ride with a tourist. Later, the Sheriff came out and asked Rex if he would sell the department gas if they looked the other way when he was speeding.

CHAPTER TWENTY-TWO
THE CATTLE BUSINESS

Dad had the foresight to see that Black Angus cattle were the coming thing in the ranching business. He kept about 50 Hereford cows, 300 or so sheep, and four to five hundred Angora goats. Synthetic material was hurting the natural fiber business, and therefore sheep and hair goat business. Most people are not that crazy about the meat- lamb and cabrieto.

The Spaniards brought Durham cattle to Texas long before it was Texas. The ones that got away and turned wild are what made the Texas Longhorn. They were so tough and hardy that they multiplied against all the odds and predators. They evolved by survival of the fittest. Over the years, they became so numerous that cowboys could rope, brand, and start a herd with the only investment of his hard work. It was an income off the land similar to the wild deer of today. The differences being a lot of sweat and blood. When the cowboys castrated the bull calves, they became sexually immature and their frame and horns kept growing with some unusually huge horns. The cowboys tried to catch the babies while the mama wasn't around. When they roped these wild cow's babies and he went to bellowing for mama, things got a little hairy. It could become a life and death situation. This is probably the main reason cowboys carried a six-shooter.

Theodore Roosevelt once made the remark that a wild Texas Longhorn could be the most dangerous game in North America. And he was a big game hunter with a world of experience. Many books have been written about capturing wild horses and cattle in Texas in those early days. Some are fiction, but based on the truth. The saying in that time, was "go West young man. Or go to Texas," because of the opportunities. There was no government and later when there was, the law was stretched very thin. There-fore, many wanted men came. The name Rangers was the state law that had to cover a lot of range. You may have heard of Judge Roy Bean-Law West of the Pecos. And Rex Ivey- (Law?) West of Terlingua Creek.

Since the Longhorns were so plentiful, they were cheap in Texas. Thus the cattle drives to the north. This was mostly in the 1860s to 1890s when Grandpa was a young man. Cowmen begin to get Hereford bulls to put on their Longhorn cows to cross breed which put a lot more meat on the calves. The Longhorn was as bony and wiry as a long-distance runner, so progress began to push out the Longhorn and concentrate on straight bred Herefords. Barbed Wire became more common after all the free range cattlemen and others had their wars. Many books and movies have been written about this.

Herefords were hardy; therefore, they used them with Long-horns. But they had their faults. Compared to Angus, these were the major differences between the Hereford and the Angus:

1. The Hereford would starve her calf before she would lose her fat reserves which had an advantage in the wild because they would rebreed.

2. Their udder and teats were not uniform and some teats would get so large that the calf could not suck it. Ranchers would have to milk them several times to get the calf to suck it.

3. They had a tendency to get pink eye, which left untreated would turn into cancer eye and cause them to go blind in that eye.

4. Their calves were usually larger at birth, sometimes resulting in death to both the mother and calf, if not found in time and assisted by the cowman.

5. Some buyers wanted purebreds and would pay less for them if the white and red hair was not in the proper places and proportions.

The Angus had almost none of these problems. Ninety percent of the cattle in Texas were Herefords in 1956 when Dad bought twelve Registered Angus cows and a bull. When he had Angus heifers large enough to enter the herd, he sold Herefords until he replaced them. When I came back to the ranch in 1962, he had about fifty head. With my job at Coleman as Assistant County Agricultural Agent, we worked with a lot of registered Hereford cattle breeders. We had first hand knowledge on improvement methods, shown from trials and experiments done on research and experiment stations across the country. So, I came with a desire to use this information on our little herd. Dad was all for it and anything else that would make life easier. To register calves and do production records by weighing them, we needed better facilities. Before this, we had to rope a cow or calf, tie her head to something, then rope her hind legs, stretch her out and pull her over with her tail. Small calves, up to about three hundred pounds, we could crowd them in a corner or rope the head and throw them by pulling a foreleg out from under them.

The first thing we did was to build new all-steel pens to hold and sort fifty head of cattle. We had never had a chute that would hold more than one cow and no squeeze chute or head gate. We built a chute to hold four head with a head gate at the end, and a set of scales at the place where they entered the chute. This was built along side of Grandpa's old horse and mule board pens, which I later converted to all steel. All of these improvements not only made work faster with a lot less sweat and cussing, but also was easier on the cattle and kept them more gentle. Near after birth, we tattooed and put a tag in the ear of each calf identifying it with its mother and the year of birth. We still did this the old fashion way since they were very small at this time. We could rope them and throw them down and tie all four feet without having to take them to the pens at the house. We still had to watch out for the mother, but the Angus were not near as likely to run over us as a long horn mama. I had set up a record system on each cow showing her sire and dam (Mom and Pop) and the offspring's sire and later the weaning weight at about 205 days of age. A few years later, we started weighing them again as yearlings. When I came back to the ranch in '62, Dad had a bull that he had bought at the Fort Worth Stock Show cattle sale. I went to The Southwest Institute near San Antonio and picked out the best three sale bulls from their Essar Herd, judging by my eye. Then went to the office to see about performance records. This was the only institution that I knew of doing performance records on Angus cattle. The Genetics department head told me that they only sold them at an annual sale. I was disappointed and told him that I had bought scales and planned on doing the same type work on our private herd.

The shorter stocky type were the kind that were popular at the stock shows, but Grandpa had always complained about them when I was showing steers. He said their neck was too short to graze grass and their legs too short to reach a cow to bred her. The ones that I had picked out to buy were taller and longer than average, and the guy said that one was the best in the performance tests. He let me buy him because I was young and going to performance test them and this is what they were pushing.

The first year of weaning weight tests on our calves, the new bull's calves weighed an average of forty eight pounds more than the show bull's calves. Consider the forty odd head of calves, that was a lot more dollars. Plus the fact that it would add up over the years of his life time and the replacement cows out of him would raise the quality of the herd.

When the computer came along, the study of genetics took a big leap. Those of us that had years of data on all of our cattle had the advantage because the percent of chances were greater that estimates were correct because there was more data to back it up. And, this percent of accuracy number was printed above every characteristic number of the animal on the registration papers. For example, a calf would weigh ten pounds more than the average. The percent chance that the estimate would be correct was right above it. More different characteristics of the calf could be evaluated because the computer made it so easy and fast to go back generations on both sides of the family tree. This information of the animal in question and both parents back several generations are shown on each registration paper making it a great selling tool. I now buy bulls with (some) genetic information taken from a hair. You can probably see that ranching and farming has progressed considerably in even my lifetime.

About 1970, Brangus cattle became popular because of the larger frame and hybrid in their calves. We purchased three quarters Brahman, one quarter Angus bulls to breed to our registered Angus cows and calve purebred Brangus offspring. The bulls we raised sold well for herd bulls and the heifers bred back to Angus also were in demand.

Typical problems ranchers have today, as in years past are many. In 2007, our area had forty inches of rain during the growing season, when we have never in my life had that much in the entire year. Grass, even in the range land pastures flourished. But the four hundred and fifty acres of fertilized introduced Klein and Coastal Bermuda grasses grew so fast that the cattle could not begin to eat it as fast as it was growing. When I reached that big 70 age, I had sold our hay baling equipment and had to hire the work done. The first cutting cost forty thousand dollars and since everyone was making hay, I couldn't sale it. It would keep several years, but with surely two more cuttings, that would be a total of one hundred twenty thousand dollars.

I asked one of my hay buyers, who buys and sales cattle to buy a hundred head of cows that would have calves soon, to add to the herd so I wouldn't have to bale so much hay. Everything still looked like such a blessing at this point. But within days after delivery, the largest catastrophe that I had ever had begin to unfold. The cattle had been purchased in the dry southern states and exposed to a deadly respiratory disease just before I received them. Not only did some of the pregnant cows get sick and die, but they all had not had time to build antibodies to protect their babies through their milk.

The cowboying begin, trying to get sick cows into the corals to be doctored and catching calves in the pasture. Some I chased horse back and some chased me. One just would not go and jumped in the pond to get away from me on Rosetta my horse. All of the cows gave birth and all of their calves got sick. Fast! Similar to the way we had to watch a herd for symptoms of Screw worms in the past, I sat and watched these calves at noon near their watering and loafing area. This was a daily job for months, because the cows I had raised contracted the disease, too. These babies were roped, doctored, marked and turned loose to go back to their mothers and most had to be caught later for another long lasting shot. Even with the best attention and medicine, half of the bought cow's calves died and some of the home raised. Some people want to out law all medicine given to animals. What looked to be the best year for this rancher, turned out to be his worst.

Talking about outlawed, it is against the law to kill a buzzard. They do clean up "road kill" and are supposed to eat nothing but dead animals. Sounds logical, only as we have mentioned, everything runs in cycles. And that includes populations of buzzards, too. When they are hungry enough, they will kill. There are years like this that I have seen many fawns, baby deer, that made a quick meal for them. When I have a bunch of young cows to calf for the first time, I have to keep them near the house in one of the three Bermuda pastures. With binoculars, I can see all over these pastures, and I do watch them many times a day. Some times it takes a little while for them to have their baby, and I have seen a hundred buzzards attack the rear of the cow and the portion of the baby exposed. They just start eating her alive, one peck at a time. I have lost five grown cows through the years, even with all my effort to prevent it. I better not say how I strive to prevent it. We have to have laws, but some times you have to go with "the boots on the ground", because you don't know the situation like they do. What would you do if you were in his boots?

As mentioned. The first baby a cow has, sometimes, takes a while and must have help. About nineteen eighty eight, I had one that I decided couldn't make it through the pelvic. When I called the nearest veterinarian, he was just coming home from a little league ball game, and turned his ankle as he was running to the house telephone. He was in pain, but said to bring her. By the time we got started, it was nearly mid night, just the two of us and the main one in pain. He shaved the hair, cut through several layers of skin and muscle to expose the body cavity. The calf in it's sack, the intestines, and the bloated stomach were all floating around a crowded area. The doctor couldn't seem to get to the calf for the huge bloated stomach, so he ask me for the scalpel. When he stabbed the stomach, it collapsed like a balloon and I wondered if he was just impatient because of the pain with his ankle. Then, he ask for needle and thread to sew up the puncture. Everything turned out fine, as did both of our grand daughters, delievered the same way. Well, nearly.

Speaking of Veterinarians, I have made it a habit of asking of their most memorable experiences. When I worked in Coleman County, the veterinarian told about having to do a C section right after he had graduated from Texas A & M. This was West Texas during a sand storm. A bad one! The cow could not get up and he did the job, by him self as I explained about with my cow, in the middle of plowed field. The sand was really blowing, and he was hovering over the exposed area, trying to keep some of the sand out. It was a hot day and he was new to the job, so he was really sweating and tense. He finally got a live calf out, the mother repaired and stood up to ease his aching back. When he looked at her rear end. There was the calf's head sticking out that he couldn't perform by standard delivery. She had had twins.

There has never been much money in cattle. When I was born in 1936, nearly half the people in America lived or worked on the farm. By the 1960s, it was less than 2% and counting part-timers, it was even less. I like to say the smarter ones were able to stay, but there was the Depression, drought, and other factors that entered into it.

CHAPTER TWENTY-THREE
HARD TIMES

Everything goes in cycles, even economic slumps. All the way through the last two centuries, the USA had a slump to cycle about every twenty years. There are all kinds of opinions as to the cause of them, usually there is a president used as a 'scapegoat'. Could it be each generation wants their kids to have it better than they did, and spoil them by not teaching them thrift? Look at the two worst. The Great Depression of 1929 to 1941 was preceded by the 'Roaring Twenties' when everyone was partying 'like there was no tomorrow, The recession of the late 1970s and 1980s with 20 percent interest rates, foreclosures, and farm sales was preceded by the Baby Boomers and irresponsible flower children's 'make love, not war.' (to stop the Communist from taking over their 43rd country) I was born in the middle of the Great Depression. What was it like?

It started with the stock market crash. Most people didn't have a job and businesses couldn't sell to people without money, so businesses and industry shut down. The farmers and ranchers were producing, but no one had money to buy their products. There was a lot of trading animals and produce for services. When the government got into it, they paid farmers for them to kill and bury cattle to reduce the surplus. Overall gross investment in the US fell from 16.2 billion in 1929 to less than 1 billion in 1932. The drought hit the farms in the West causing the 'Dust Bowl', which put the hurt on farmers and sent many to the city. The film 'Grapes of Wrath' shows how bad it was.

At least in the cities, they had soup lines so they would not starve. Notice how thin people were in the pictures taken during that time. There were scenes that looked like those you have seen of starving people after disasters around the world.

The Civilian Conservation Corps was established under the Roosevelt administration for building all kinds of public works such as parks, in order to put people to work and get money circulating again. The men worked for one dollar a day! That was big pay in those days. The Tennessee Valley Authority built dams for flood control and hydroelectric power, so those without a job and thought that seeking charity was humiliating were eager to sign up. So many of them had been well-off middle class. With the exception of the dust bowl farmer, the country people were probably better off than their city cousins. Like the popular country song, "A country boy can survive."

The late 1920's was a perilous time for banks, especially in rural areas where only a constable or marshall patrolled a large territory. Texas banks were being robbed at a rate of three or four a day. In the fall of 1927, the Texas Bankers Association declared it would pay $5,000 to anybody who killed an individual caught in the act of robbing a bank. To clear up any misunderstanding this might have caused, the association added that it would not pay a single penny for live robbers. This was the kind of retribution, the old-timers said, that the criminal mind could understand.

During the depression, this old house was home to the Elkins family of six. It was very old then because Grandpa had farm hands live in it during the mule and horse-farming seasons of the past. At that time, it was two separate houses. This picture was taken June 2010 and reminds me of the fun I had there visiting the four neighbor boys. Their milk cow would use the free grazing down our county road and many times be near our house by the time the bus brought us from school. Several of us smaller boys would ride her the mile back to this house. We hunted squirrels and small rabbits with the slingshots that we had made from a forked stick and inner tube tire rubber. They were expert shots and hunted with earnest because that was usually the only meat they had. They nearly always hit the target in the head so it wouldn't bruise the meat. Without the meat, it was cornbread and milk from that old cow. I can remember how bad the old house looked even back then. It had only single board walls with lots of cracks, no electricity or water, a wood cook stove and heater. One of the older boys was club-footed from birth and had a hard time keeping up with the others. A club foot is a deformity with the foot drawn up tight. Before they moved, Dad found some way to get an operation for him.

Years later, Dad was plowing the field below this old house and a car stopped on the county road and a soldier walked through the deep plowed ground to the tractor. It was this young man that had the operation wanting to show Dad what it had meant to his life. He was able to be accepted into the Army and raise his standard of living to a degree that he had never dreamed of.

Even as late as the 1970s with 20% interest rates, there were a great many farms that went out of business. Farming and ranching is like most businesses. It takes a lot of capital and an understanding banker to throw all that fertilizer out on the ground hoping for rain and a lot of other factors necessary to make a profit. I was teaching Agriculture in Lometa, beginning a family, but still wanting to make my entire living off of the ranch. Between predators and prices, there just wasn't a future in the wool of sheep and hair of goats. This isn't farming country and I sure can't sing, so I figured options to supplement beef cows might be chickens, dairy or hogs. I chose what I disliked the least, hogs and spent the next two years researching the business. I contacted the Agriculture Extension Service in the adjoining states to get an address of their best hog operations, and then went to see them. The poultry and dairy industry had advanced in modern technology much more than the swine industry. Therefore, I incorporated some of all three into my plans. I knew that the money to build the facilities would be hard to come by so I spent a lot of time and lost a lot of sleep dreaming of the ideal plan. Some times, I couldn't sleep and would get up and do more sketches and contemplate different scenarios.

To make a long story short, I designed a complete farrow to finish, completely slatted floor and air-conditioned farrowing house, nursery, and finishing house. I built outside pens for boars (males) and four pens for pregnant sows (females) with shelters and sprinklers for summer time. These were used for breeding and gestation, then each group of sows were to be brought in just before they delivered their babies. With all the information and plans, I couldn't get the Farm Home Association (FHA) to loan me the money. My banker friend insisted that I call my congressman. He said that was FHA's business to help a young person get started. Even then, it took awhile to get through all the red tape.

The congressman wrote back in a few days and said that he had researched and found that I didn't have enough experience and knowledge. I wrote him back and thanked him, I told him that

I had many generations of agriculture before me and I had been a County Agricultural Agent that advised ranchers and farmers similar to this. About three days later the FHA agent called and said let's review your case. I only got one-third of what it would take to build it. Therefore, I had to do all the welding and building myself and pay the rest as I went along. The people that sold me the feed processing mill installed it, but I put up the grain bins, augers to the mill, feeders, and built farrowing crates and virtually everything else. The 120-foot by 30-foot totally slatted floor finishing house with scales in the loading chute was the last addition. Dad said, "When are you EVER going to get through with this thing?" My two little boys, Mike and Kirk, were old enough to help. Mary wouldn't let me use Lisa. She didn't want even a hint of hog smell on her little girl.

This took several years because I was still teaching, farming and ranching.. By the time it was complete, it was like none that I had seen. I took sixty to seventy finished hogs to the packing plant in San Antonio, Texas every two weeks, totaling around fifteen hundred head a year. At this time, I was in the top 10% in the USA in numbers produced on one farm. When I quit twenty-five years later, I was in the bottom 10% because everyone was building units like mine. If I had just started designing and contracting to build these facilities, I would not have had to put up with the stinking things.

I filled out a date book diary a year in advanced, so everyday, I could open the book and see if it was time to put the boars with the next group of sows, wean, go from nursery to finishing house, sale or what. I literally went by the book and what Texas A&M recommended. It worked! Every two months, a new batch of nearly three hundred pigs would be born, and others shifted through the houses. Every two weeks, I would haul the load of fat hogs in a big tandem dual wheeled trailer that I built to a packing plant in San Antonio. Once before the kids were born, I left Mary at her folks in Coleman while I went to buy boars. When I got back, she said that she guessed I had forgotten about our anniversary. I am used to checking that date book for about everything, but I didn't have it with me. A quick thought came and I told her, "Oh no! Come out and I will show you the gift that I got you. Just pick you one of those boar hogs." I had to take her out to dinner.

I have never hired help except on occasions. My two sons had chores and got an education from the work and money for college. We made enough in the twenty-five years with hogs to raise and educate the three kids and put the cow money into land that I had bought from cousins. The reason I quit is because the big packing companies bought out all the smaller packing companies and shut them down. Trucking to the nearest packing plant in northern Mississippi was too expensive.

It was so labor efficient that I raised my registered Angus cattle on the home ranch and three thousand acres of leased land, baled my own hay for the cattle, bought the grain from the farmer, made my own feed from it, turned it into finished product and delivered to the packer myself. I had quit teaching before I got to this point. This cut out the middlemen and made it a much more profitable operation. Today, these factory hog farms are so huge because of modern technology that they have over-built and driven down prices. Chickens and hogs are very efficient compared to cattle feeding, but if feed gets too expensive for the cattle, they can eat grass that the chickens and hogs can't. If there weren't cattle, all the grass on all the land not suited for farming in America would go to waste. Therefore, considering resources used, cattle are free, and using renewable resources. No one should fuss about that except the Global Warming folks that claim their breathing is melting the glaciers.

The only farming that I was doing was baling my hay and some of my neighbors' hay. Instead of horses and mules, like Dad and Grandpa used, I had one small tractor, implements, and a big four wheel drive 4430 John Deere. It had a cab, air, windshield wipers, radio, all kinds of hydraulics, tilt and telescoping steering wheel, and a seat with thirty settings. With the new round baler, I got a monitor to put in the cab that showed everything going on with the baler. This tractor is thirty years old, too. Now, they have much more! Ground Positioning Satellite to control the amounts of fertilizer, seed, etc. So the better soils get more fertilizer and seed than the poorer soils. Automatically! Harvesting machines for all crops are so high tech that it would take pages to describe.

I had been selling feed for a company, baling hay in the neighborhood, leasing ranches and increasing the size of the herd, so I still had plenty to do after I quit teaching. From the beginning, we had been selling Registered breeding herd bulls and females the year around. My wife didn't want me to quit teaching because she didn't think we could make it with out that big check. After I did, and I would come in all dirty and sweating, she would ask "How much did you make TODAY".

CHAPTER TWENTY-FOUR
GRASS FARMERS

Cousin Merlin McAnelly had been leasing me our Ivey grand-
parent's ranch. He told me that he would give me his Nix ranch
lease free if I would take care of his cows on the Bend place. His
father was a descendant of Robert McAnelly 1830 who was the
father of the first white child born in Lampasas County. This is
on a historical marker on the Bend highway, Texas 580, right by
the ranch known as McAnelly Bend. The community is named for
the bend in the Colorado River. Merlin and I continue to be good
friends after these seventy-odd years. Once about four years ago,
he wanted to sell calves from the Bend ranch. I told him to come
out to the ranch early before it got so hot. Well, the sun had been
up several hours before he came from his home in Brady. I said, "I
have waited this long for a doctor in his office, but never in a cow
pasture." He handed me a coke-cooler with these words on it – on
time is when I get there!

My leased places were at Long Cove, Moline, Nix and Bend.
All about ten to fifteen miles away. The largest one that I leased
was my mother's home place that I leased from her sister, and later,
her son, Doctor Merlin McAnelly. Merlin and I were born a week

apart and were raised like twins. The Ivey ranch and one joining it on the far side were about three thousand acres. We had an old fashioned cattle drive twice a year to drive them each spring to the improved summer pastures on the home place. Then again in the fall to take them back to the winter pastures that had been rested and allowed to grow during the summer.

Through the years, a lot of kids that liked to ride horses got to go on the drive, and one of them was Lisa. She had loved horses almost from day one. The boys didn't, they rode trail bikes, but Lisa and I were born with this love of horses. I do believe in God-given talents and vocations. The last two miles to home were down a road but most of it was open range on big ranches with no fences on the sides. There usually were cattle that wanted to get with ours and we had to keep them driven back. Then we would look up and here they were coming again. With a couple hundred or more cows scattered out in a long line, it was a chore to watch it all and keep the bunches from getting together. The trail bikes didn't get winded running up and down the sides like the horses, so they were pretty handy. This was before three-wheelers, or later 4-wheelers, became popular.

The other leases were smaller, and I hauled the cattle on the big tandem dual wheel hog trailer. The grass I was hauling them to was the four hundred fifty acres of cropland that I had put in permanent grass. Farming is so expensive and our fields were not as good as some, so

I planted them all in permanent improved grasses. It consumes half the profit in the grass to bale it for hay, so I let the cows do that job for free. At the same time, the range grasses on the leased ranches were growing and making winter standing hay that the cows could harvest and I wouldn't have to handle it. I just had to feed protein cubes to supplement it in the winter and that is much easier and less expensive. The bottom line is what is important in any kind of business.

We cut the fields up into smaller 'cells,' pastures with electric fences, in order to rotate the cows and let the other cells recuperate and grow. Texas A&M proved this to be a much more efficient way of getting the most grazing and also maintain a good stand of grass. The cow's manure is spread more evenly over the cells since they are so concentrated and the hoof action disturbs the ground enough to plant the many little seeds. The manure spread like this makes it unnecessary to fertilize with commercial fertilizer every year. About half of the ranch field acreage, we put in Klein grass, which comes earlier and stays later than the coastal Bermuda that the rest of the pastures were established in. The Coastal Bermuda is hardier in the dry, hot part of the summer. This system takes more time and management of knowing when to move the cattle and to check the water troughs and electric fences. Fertilize and spraying for weeds are expensive, but a very important for the Bermuda. Especially selling good clean hay. I always made some hay every year, and the years that it rained more, we made a lot.

It sounds like we were making money hand over fist, but it takes a lot of money to repair and maintain hay baling equipment, or pay someone to cut, rake, bale, and haul it. What I was doing is working eighty to ninety hours a week like my rancher forefathers. Everyone up the line from the producer, in all farming businesses, make much more profit than the one who produces the product. Seems like most of them get rich by the time they are 60 years old and retire, but we have no retirement and have to work until we die. If we work hard and smart enough, we will buy the home place from the other heirs. So far, each generation has kept this ranch in the family. This was always on my mind.

Speaking of dying, farming is in the top three most dangerous occupations in America. Personally, I have been thrown on my head many times or knocked off the horse by tree limbs while chasing cattle. I have been kicked all over by cows and bulls. My dad ran over me with a pickup truck in the pasture, and my car was hit by a freight train going to teach school one morning. Most of my accidents were caused by doing things in too big of a hurry. With all the accidents mentioned above, I have had many bones broken, cut, burns, and mashed fingers. Examples: Most frequently is getting a gate kicked into the body or head by a cow. I have had stitches on my head several times from this and mashed fingers. Once when I was pregnancy-testing cows, and the boy working the head gate couldn't get her out of the alley, I stepped out of the box behind the squeeze chute and yelled at her. With no warning, she charged and slammed me into a two-inch steel pipe gate, almost knocking me unconscious. I was on my knees trying to get blood back to my brain, when the boy yelled, "Look out, Mr. Herring! She's coming back down the alley!" I scrambled back to the box behind the squeeze chute to get away from her. There were six cows in the chute behind me that I had forgot about, and when I swung the gate from them to shut the mad cow out, the six cows saw light at the end of the tunnel and ran over me getting out. The squeeze chute is narrower at the bottom, so they all stepped on me on their way out. There were no broken bones or stitches necessary this time, but some pretty sore muscles. I had a bull buyer coming that afternoon, so I had to change clothes and clean the bloody places on my head before he came. Didn't want him to think that I had bad cattle. He might not have wanted one of my bulls.

The scariest accident was when I had separated several cows from their calves and came back later to pair them with the real mothers. They were older calves, and I wasn't sure who belonged to whom. When the calf gets hungry, he will go to mom to nurse, and she won't deny him. I could bend forward and sneak up from the rear to catch the calf while his head was buried in his mom's flank sucking. She started to move, and I charged to catch the calf's hind leg before he saw me. She stopped and laid me out backwards with a quick right jab of the hind foot to my forehead. It felt like I had been electrocuted. Fire went down the nerves in both arms and legs! I couldn't move a finger or anything! I lay there on the ground a mile from home by myself, scared that my neck was broken, and I would be paralyzed for life. The longer I lay there, the more disgusted I became with myself for being in too big of a hurry and careless. Quite awhile later, I was able to roll on my stomach, and then later get up. When I got to the pickup truck, it took a while to get the door open and get in. I could barely get my hands high enough to reach the steering wheel. I then decided to lie down in the seat and wait until I felt safe to drive home. I was lucky again, no permanent damage. A friend, Donny Bell, told me that he bet that my guardian angel would be so happy when his job of watching over me was finished. Now that I am pretty old, and I do have aches when I first get up, but the most trouble is from all the dust that I breathed in the hog barns and the cattle lots. With that many cattle stirring up the dust, one could hardly see. Even when I stop for a gate, I open the door and the door just funnels the dust that is catching up into the cab.

Through it all, I have thanked the Lord many times that he put me here in this part of Texas on this ranch with a desire to do this kind of work. You just have to have the hard times to really enjoy the good ones!

After I quit the hog business, I rebuilt the swine facilities from the ground up to make much larger cattle pens, chutes, alleys, and scales - the one I was using in the preceding story were too small. To have a Certified Bangs Free Herd, we had to collect blood from each animal every year and have it tested. The Braham bulls we used on our cows to get Brangus calves just did not want to go in that chute again each year. The old pens had one large pen and I had to put them in the chute. You have probably seen the rodeo bulls, cowboys ride? How would you like to make one do something they didn't want to do? Each year, I sharpened a hay pitch fork and faced him head on. Each would bow that big neck, paw the ground and dare me. It would make the hair stand up on the back of the neck! Had to be done, though. One jab in the nose with the pitch fork would do the trick. This was a strong incentive for the new pens.

I put the hog-finishing house, with the insulation under the tin, over the cattle working area to make it a little more pleasant when we worked the cattle and provide shelter over the feed troughs and cattle in that area. Two of the pens in this area had permanent feed troughs with a concrete floor under the shed and with exercise area and water troughs outside.

Also, we had two larger pens where I could hold a hundred-odd head in each pen and get them into the big alley to sort or go down a chute to the squeeze chute. From there, they could be sorted to five pens or turned out the side. Or go over the new digital scales. Two of the optional sorting pens mentioned can be used as sick pens because they are smaller and on the other side of the big alley and chute, off to themselves with water and sheds. The two large pens, mentioned, are where the cattle are brought in from the pastures, and they have large self-feeders where we can wean calves from their mothers. One has a long auger that I could send feed from the feed mill room. I fed the 'for sale' bulls by hand in the trough from a cart in the alley to keep them from getting too fat.

All of this has a six and a half foot tall oilfield pipe fencing around it with the pens and fifty gates made the same way. No matter how upset an animal is, once I get them into it, there is no getting out, unless someone forgets to close a gate. All those gates make it easier and quicker to handle cattle. One person can do most anything by himself. The squeeze chute even has a self-catching head gate on it.

From 1992 to 2000, I was County Commissioner from my precinct, and was so busy that I hired a welder to build these facilities. I had taught him how to weld when he was in my Agricultural shop classes, and he went on to make a vocation of it. I had done all the construction of the swine facilities and other cattle pens up to this point, even portable chutes for several of my leased ranches. I had built flat beds for the dual wheel pickups, two sizes of flat bed trailers, three sizes of livestock trailers and a six-yard dump trailer. Also we kept a one ton dual wheel truck with PTO, air, hydraulics and wench to pull the larger trailers and a four-wheel drive three-quarter ton with a cube feeder to put out protein cubes in the pastures in all kinds of weather.

We started baling hay with poor used equipment, but soon decided it was more economical to have better equipment so it wouldn't break down at a time when the hay needed to be harvested—or in the middle of harvest. All of this took a pretty good shop with tools to do repairs. My Christmas presents were usually tools. Now we use the old hog-farrowing house as a bigger and better shop. I built my first grader blade and three-point hookup for the old Farmall H tractor, and then a forklift, post driver and all kinds of equipment. Now that I am nearly too old to use it, I have a dream shop with tools for nearly any farm repair job.

Our boys, when they were home, helped with a lot of the building. One son is the purchasing officer for Willbanks Metals in Fort Worth, and the other son is a design Mechanical Engineer for Weir SPM in Fort Worth. It looks like they enjoyed this part of the farm the best. Lisa is in public relations at the state office of the Texas Department of Public Safety. Maybe watching the boys and their fast cars influenced her in this direction.

Ranchers are really farmers. The livestock do the harvesting. Ranchers are also conservationists because if you don't take care of your grass and soil, it won't continue to take care of you. This can happen within months! This involves keeping out trees and brush, except just enough for shade and wildlife, and rotating livestock off of pastures to keep them from eating the grass so short that it leaves the ground naked to the elements. If the soil is left naked, a single rain can cost you a thousand years of soil. Even without the 'big rain,' the soil will not retain and absorb the water. It will just run off and not provide the moisture necessary for the grass to grow. This is the most frequent and important mistake that some ranchers make.

My dad was a director of the Hill Country Soil and Water Conversation District Board since it was formed in the 1940s and was the first chairman of the board. I was elected to the board after he retired from it. We have felt a great love of the land, as well as of the USA, and believe this work is something we can give back. Besides, it will help our rancher neighbors to make a success in their business. God put good grasses that livestock prefer on the land first. Then, if for some reason, usually man, the grass was not allowed to mature and seed over a period of years,' He' had a grass come up that the livestock didn't like as well. If this continued, He had weeds and brush take over. The weeds die in the winter and leave the ground naked, and the brush or cedar will shade the ground so that grass can't grow.

When the ground is bare, a raindrop hits the ground with enough speed that it is like a small bomb. It makes a crater and throws the soil up in the air and when it comes down in the water, it has started its trip to the Gulf of Mexico. On the other hand, if there is a good stand of grass, not grazed too short, the grass leaves cushion the fall and lets the raindrop down easy. The water follows the leaves down the stem and roots into the underground water reserves. If the water does get to the ground in between the grasses, the leaves act as a barrier to hold it back until the water can be absorbed. If a rancher is to make a success, he must keep a good thick stand of the better grasses. The better grasses put on more pounds on the cattle, and the thick stand of grass absorbs and retains more water for the dry times to grow more grass. These two sentences are far more important than the 'quality' of the cattle.

You hear a lot these days from non-farmers about 'Sustainable Agriculture.' Like the story of 'Chicken Little' – "the sky is falling, the sky is falling!" Global Warming, Green this and that, Natural Fertilizer, and Natural Meat. The truth is, everything from the weather on this planet to everything on it goes in cycles. People that live in and of nature watch it, study it as well as the scientists do. Some people are against commercial fertilizer, but some countries fertilize with human manure. America has higher standards and more oversight on their products than any country in the world. I try not to buy imported products when there is a choice, and I sure don't want my food from any other country! 'Natural' and 'Green' buzzwords are baloney. Name one thing on this planet that doesn't come from the ground or water!

Some people don't even know where their food comes from. Animal rights people want us all to be vegetarians. God was the first one to kill an animal to use the skin to cover Adam and Eve's nakedness, and the animal did not have a natural death because there was no such thing as death in the Garden of Eden. Like the Good Shepherd, Jesus said, "I know my sheep and they know me." We are the good shepherds with those we are responsible for. Ask any real rancher for the truth on livestock care. He will put his animals first 24 hours a day, 7 days a week, 52 weeks a year even if he has to miss a meal or a ball game. If that first calf heifer is having a baby on the coldest, wettest night of the year, nothing will stand in the way of helping her. Global Warming people say more energy is used farming, thus pollution comes from farming. Animal Rights people say don't eat animals. So what are they going to eat? Each other? Maybe so, if we do as they say! We will go back to the cave-man days.

Sustainable agriculture has been going on since God kicked Adam out of the Garden of Eden. How many thousands of years has that been? American farmers increase the 'all time annual pro-duction' records at least every decade. The people that really 'care for the animals' are ranchers and hunters. Since we see and take care of the animals more than a city person does their pets, we want to meet all their needs. For instance, one day a Northern cold front brought a wall of water (rain) across a pasture by our house, and the just-weaned calves were scared to death of the rain and all ran to our house wanting protection. Other times that we have had cattle near the house, thunder and lightening would bring the cattle to us. When an animal gets trapped, hurt or sick, we are their saviors, and they know it.

Dad taught me to talk to my cows. Do so with a calm assuring tone. When they are about to spook at something, or afterwards, it will calm them and help the situation. Grandpa told how cow-boys would sing to the herd at night on the trail to Kansas. Dad and I call cows with a long loud howl to get their attention, and then "suck, suck, suck.' When up close, we didn't have to do the howl. Working in the pens, we used this if they got a little excited. Dad also used it on me. From 95 to 100% of the time, we didn't use a whip or hotshot. Cattle don't move until you get in their space, the 'flight zone.' How fast they move depends on how fast you enter it. We move closer to get them to move and stop, or step back if they move too fast. The problem we have using auction barn help is, they are too loud and too fast. Most of the time, easy does it, is faster. When I was younger, Dad would get upset with me when I got upset with the cattle. He would blame it on the Ivey genes and say, "That's the Ivey blood cropping out in you."

A few years ago, I took some old cows to the cattle auction in San Saba, Texas but forgot to get the identification tag numbers from each cow to record in the herd book. The next morning as I was walking down the auction alley looking for my cows, they saw me first, recognized me, and began to "Low," a depressed moo sound. They were looking and speaking to me as if to say, "Get me out of here!" That depressed me as much as having to put one out of her misery. I got to thinking about it and realized why they looked up to me. I had taken care of them from birth to old age! Some I had helped deliver them at birth, and some I had helped to deliver their first baby.

First calf heifers have trouble at delivery, occasionally, but nearly never after the first birth. Usually a rancher will pitch a rope on the heifer and tie her to the pickup, then try to shorten the slack until she can move very little. When he begins to put the surgical chains on the baby's front legs, usually still inside with only the head showing, she stops moving around. Then, he positions the calf puller device and hooks the chains to the puller jack. At this point, pulling down, it doesn't take but a moment to complete, if there is no major problem. It is very necessary to turn her loose and get out of the way as soon as possible, so she will bond with the baby calf.

One time, I had just turned the heifer loose and my Great Pyrenees Guard dog came running up to check things out. He was a huge white dog that I had running with the goat herd to protect them from predators. The heifer had not seen the dog before, and she spooked and ran off from her newborn. I tried everything to get her back to the calf and accept it, but she never realized that it was hers. I had to raise it on a bottle. Rarely do ranchers have other complications and have to take them to a chute or even a veterinary clinic. Any animal mother, as soon as the baby is born, will clean the nose and mouth first to clear the air passage way. Next, chew the umbilical cord or naval cord loose about six inches from the body. She then stimulates the blood flow thereby warming the baby by licking it clean all over. All these procedures are done with a human baby by the doctor and in the same order. Except the chewing the cord in two and the licking. This is called 'animal intuition' – the immediate knowing something without conscious use of reasoning. (Like the actions of teen-agers) Adults figure things out with their God given brain and animals have 'animal intuition' that is also given by God.

It is hard to kill your horse, but sometimes it has to be done. The last one that I had to shoot was born in a pasture just south of our house and raised near our yard fence. We have kept our horses here because it is handy to catch them there. My daughter, Lisa, was just a very small girl, and she grew up with the colt feeding him table scraps and favors across the fence. He was a very well bred and flashy horse, but was still a spoiled pet that was not the best cow horse that I had ever had.

Three nights a year at the local FFA youth invitational rodeo, I helped with the Grand Entry.

We start the rodeo with the music and flags and I lead the kids out first. I rode Red because everyone thought he was so pretty.

Red, like his owner, lead a hazardous life. Before the horse shoer, Jamie Smart came, I tied him up short to a limb above his head. It was a while before Jamie came, and I noticed a mare was visiting with him under the tree. Wasn't saying much, just standing there. When Jamie drove up, the mare, wheeled and ran off. Red must have forgotten that he was tied and started to run, but when he hit the end of the rope, all his weight and power drove a broken limb two inches in diameter into his head. He was bleeding terribly, but we got the trailer and headed to Marble Fall to a horse specialist. The stick had broken off in his forehead and was sticking out about a foot. Looked like a Unicorn. The Veterinarian put him in a padded room and told me that he might die when he pulled it out. He didn't, but the Doc. had to clean out the bark that was left in the hole, and he said he could feel the membrane that enclosed the brain. It was that close to killing him instantly. He got over this, but it did change his personality.

Red stuck a piece of metal in the upper part of his hoof when he was fairly young, and even though we got the infection cured, the hoof was damaged for the rest of his life. Many trips to the veterinary clinics couldn't make it right. I had a special shoe changed regularly, but it got worse over a long period of time. Lisa had gone to college and maybe she didn't realize the pain that Red was in, when she said, "Daddy, don't shoot Red." I would see him standing alone raising and lowering that hoof all the time, and doctors had given up on him. After making the decision not to have him injected and put to sleep and then have to drag him with a tractor to be burned up, I decided to do it myself. I dug the grave with the tractor, loaded Red in a low livestock trailer to take his last ride. Through the years, I have put screwworm eaten and injured animals out of their misery many times, so I know just where to shoot to make an instant humane kill. I unloaded Red, lead him into the hole, said good-bye and shot him. It was even harder to tell Lisa, but thankfully, she was mature enough to understand. The horse I rode most of the time while I was in school, was also named Red, but we had others in between the two Reds.

Ranchers deal with death all year long, every year. They watch and help their animals grow up and become attached to some individuals, but we know the reality of the purpose God put them on this earth. When their usefulness is over, they are used for food. If we treated them as humans and buried them all like humans, every foot of land on this planet would be a graveyard. Pilgrims learned that some Indians put a dead fish in a hole with each corn seed for fertilizer. With our animals, we run the corn through the animal and use their manure to fertilize the grass or grain. The animal is eaten by man and their waste is eventually used for fertilizer. Everything is a cycle! The 'new' term so popularly used and so Politically Correct is 'Sustainable Agriculture.' An old rancher friend of mine, Bill Wittenburg, was about to die and told his family that it was time for him to make room for others. He knew and understood the cycle.

Farm and ranch folks are more conservative, as a whole, than their city cousins. I believe this is because they see the big picture instead of a more narrow or focused one. I don't see how a person raised on a ranch could not believe in God, His word, and the cycles. Now, my boys live in Dallas and Fort Worth, and my daughter in Austin because we can't all make a living here on the ranch. When this country boy goes to town to see them, I can see why they have to drive like the devil and act like him sometimes. A small town in rural southwest Texas has a sign on either side coming in that reads "This is God's Country – Don't Drive through it Like Hell." In the big cities, I realize my kids have to drive that way, but hopefully, they will remember their roots and not act like the devil.

There are good people in the cities, though. When my little girl went to work at the Naval Academy, just east of Washington, DC, I was very fearful and told her boss so. They couldn't have been better. For instance, when the roads were icy, they knew that she was not used to driving on icy roads, and sent someone to drive her to work. Country folks are politically conservative like our founding fathers were when they formed the constitution and set up our country as a Republic instead of a Democracy. Under a democracy, majority rules, even if it is just barely a majority. Under a republic, supreme power rests in ALL citizens! We country people are a very small percent of voters, so you see why we will fight for our republic. I was once persuaded to run for County commissioner and served for two terms, but I would nearly as soon live in New York City as make a profession of it.

CHAPTER TWENTY-FIVE
SMALL CITY AND SCHOOL LIFE BACK THEN

Speaking of cities, our nearest town is Lometa. It is about ninety miles north of Austin and ninety miles west of Waco. It is about twenty miles to the nearest other little town. July 25, 1885 the Santa Fe Railroad bought land and plotted a town site for the future town of Lometa, Texas. The railroad had bypassed the village of Senterfitt, three miles to the west. Senterfitt was a thriving stagecoach stop, cattle trail stopover and in general, a typical western town with hotels and saloons. The residents lost little time moving businesses and people to the new town. Leading men and women of the town barred the building of a saloon because Senterfitt had been much like Dodge City, Kansas when a trail herd came by.

Eight men, including John Nance who was Grandpa's brother-in-law, formed a law enforcement group to rid the community of the bad element of men, or force them to obey the law. They carried a pistol on their belt and a rifle on their saddle. One was a Harvey Maxwell, a former Texas Ranger who was attacked at a church camp meeting but he shot and killed the man. The outlaw period lasted about fifteen years. Fortunately, the eight members of the group had a strong sense of right and never turned into a vigilante group as in neighboring San Saba, just twenty miles west of Lometa.

Following the Civil War, the law in the Texas Hill country was stretched thin. Vigilante committees arose to protect land and property, but many of those secretive groups turned into violent mobs, and through violence and intimidation created a reign of terror over the area for over two decades until 1896 to 1899, when a band of citizens with the help of the Texas Rangers, succeeded in ending the mob's rule. Many had lost their land, and at least forty three men had lost their lives at the hands of the "San Saba Mob."

Railroads won the West, and towns had sprung up everywhere the railroad went. Lometa was more important than most other small towns because the railroad built a large lake to supply the water for the steam engines.

The north boundary of the watershed for the lake started on the mountain on the Herring ranch. The water was pumped to the big steel tanks that were by the tracks and the round house.

The round house was a huge tall building for servicing and repairs on the big steam engines, and it contained a turntable to reverse the direction of travel of the big steam engines. Thus, the name ROUND HOUSE. Repairs to tracks were performed mostly with hammers and bars, so it took a lot of people in the Lometa area to keep the tracks and right a ways in good shape. It was hard work, and it took tough men to do it. I'm sure that is why the city fathers wouldn't let the saloons move in.

As it was, it took a pretty tough City Marshal or Deputy to keep the peace, and there are a lot of stories about them. One big worker was doped up on something and was causing all kinds of trouble. When the Officer got there, the man tried to kill him and was shot six times with his 'forty-five.' Another time, a group was going to run the Officer out of town, so they sent a man to locate him. When they found the Officer, he was pushing buck shot cartridges into a 12 gauge pump shot gun. They decided not to try to run him out of town.

This Officer was T.R. Gholson, who later became County sheriff. His Grandfather was B.F.(Frank) Gholson who was a Texas Ranger in the late 1850's and '60's. Frank was a member of a patrol in 1858 which recaptured two children, Tobe and Rebecca Jackson from Indians near the present city of Sweetwater. They had been two weeks tracking the Indians from Lampasas County.

His most famous action was when he took part in the Battle of Pease River. In this battle, Cynthia Ann Parker, a white woman and wife of Chief Nacoma, was recaptured twenty four years after she had been taken by Comanches in a raid on Fort Parker. Gholson was in Sul Ross's company. No, it really was not John Wayne that recued her.

A one hundred mile railway was built from the main line to Eden, Texas from 1910 to 1913. It made a T into the main line by the Jess Pickett ranch going west by the Herring ranch. So the south boundary of the Pickett and Herring ranches was the Eden railroad and the east boundary was the main Santa Fe. Line. The mountain range on the north and later the State Highway 183 on the south were the other boundries. Most cattle were shipped on the railroads. Remember, we mentioned Pickett and Herring driving cattle to Kansas for shipping East by rail, and now, it comes right by the ranches. Lometa had a large set of cattle pens and dipping vats where cattle were assembled from the area from trucks or on hoof to be sent by rail. At one time, two trainloads were shipped to the Brown's ranch in Wyoming, which at that time was the most shipped at one time on the Santa Fe. The Eden branch railroad line brought cattle from the west and sand from the river country to bed the floors of the cattle cars. The pens were across the tracks from the depot there in downtown Lometa.

Passenger trains were a major mode of transportation in those days, and many were from all walks of life and dressed very differently from the local people. Cowboys and others liked to meet the regular scheduled trains as they disembarked for a meal or simply a rest stop. This was an education for both the locals and the city folks.

As automobiles became larger and more powerful, many people rode buses. Farm pickups could only haul one cow or horse before trailers were common. Most livestock was hauled on flatbed trucks with sideboards and semi-trucks were much smaller than the ones today in 2010. Today, ranchers have gooseneck trailers pulled by powerful pickups that will haul as much as the old semi-trucks did. The modern semi-trucks took much of the hauling of all kinds of produce away from the railroad, but the railroads shifted to other products, and they carry more freight than ever.

In 1912 the Scholton brother's Narrow Gauge Railway met the Santa Fe at Lometa.

This privately owned railroad was used to haul cedar posts from cedar brakes in southern San Saba County to the main line in Lometa. They had a bridge across the Colorado River below Bend that was washed out several times in floods. It was a business done on a large scale, but only lasted eight years. The Eden branch by the Herring ranch is still in operation today.

Lometa is in Lampasas County. Lampasas County was created in 1856 and was on the edge of vast Western frontier where Bison still roamed. The Civil War began five years later and diverted law and order from the area. Lampasas is said to have gained the reputation of being one of the roughest places in Texas. The city of Lampasas was created because the Indians had been using the smelly sulfur springs for healing powers for years. The town was formed and many hotels and businesses thrived because of the springs. The

1870s were the most lawless time for the county. Indians, outlaws, and rustlers were a threat to life and property. Bulford Cox killed a total of 27 men, the first in a Lampasas saloon. He lost part of an ear in this fight. After this fight, he took up with the Pink Higgins bunch and experienced a lot of running gun battles on horseback between the two groups. The most famous was the Higgins and Horrell feud. It started in a saloon in Lampasas in 1873 and lasted for five years. Sheriffs were shot, state police were brought in, and several men of both families were killed before it was ended.

Pink Higgins and R.A. Mitchell on their return from a trip up the Cattle Trail. Bottom: Felix Castello, Jess Standard, R.A. Mitchell, and Pink Higgins. Top: Powell Woods, unidentified, Buck Allen, A.T. Mitchell. (W.P. Webb Papers, Barker Texas History Center)

There were very large nice homes in Lometa built on Main Street going east with the schools at the end and on top of the hill.

As mentioned before, there were many one-room school houses within walking distances from homes, scattered all over the present day school district. A larger school was built in Lometa, and a so-called College for the kids from the one-room schools that wanted to go beyond the first few grades.

Many of those students had to room and board with someone that lived in the immediate area and in some cases, the parents moved to town and commuted to the farm. Remember, the typical school bus was a privately owned horse and wagon. I remember my mother telling about being the school bus driver when she and her neighbors were going to a two-room school at the Long Cove community. Once when the first 'dust bowl' day's dust storm was coming into the area, the teacher sent the kids home because it was getting dark in the middle of the day. The black clouds were boiling and had almost made it look like night. The kids were scared that it was the end of the world! Mother was the older of the kids, and said she whipped that poor old horse through open pastures, crossing creeks delivering kids to their homes and getting her little brothers home before the dust hit them.

During the Civil War, my great-grandfather William Giles Herring served in Company K, 8th Regiment 12th Texas. Later, he was on the school board of Clear Creek School east of Lometa. My father, Fred Herring, was the president of the school board when the present school was built in Lometa in 1942. It is a large long building that took the place of the others with grades one through twelve

Lometa High School

It still is a lovely building made of limestone with a hall from north to south. Students started first grade at the north end and worked their way through the grades back and forth across the hallway until they finished the twelve grades at the south end. Actually, on the south end, there were subject matter rooms. Later a gym and cafeteria were added, and after that until the present, other specialty buildings were built.

After the passenger and freight trains ceased to stop and high tech equipment took the place of manual labor on the tracks, the town dwindled from over two thousand to the present population of seven hundred fifty. Since it is about twenty miles to the nearest town, the town with a good school and the bare necessities has stabilized. If the cost of fuel continues to go up, there may be more little towns like Lometa with Mom and Pop stores returning. The old false front buildings on Main Street still remain with about half still in use. Occasionally, a Yankee-looking tourist will be seen taking pictures of the old buildings with the ranchers pickup trucks parked in front, and maybe a dog in the back.

One day a certain character from down near the Colorado River, well-it was R J Henniger, had a hay baler behind his pickup and wanted a cup of coffee, so he just jumped his old pickup up on the sidewalk all the way to the wall in order to get the baler out of the middle of the street. Several years ago, there was a fight between two old men in their sixties in the middle of the street. There was a long line of pickups with goats in their trailers waiting in line to get to the livestock auction, and they had blocked this business owner's entrance. The owner of the business came out and started telling the wrong old rancher what he should do. He got a little heated and piled out of his pickup and the fight was on. Sure wish one of those Yankee tourists had been there with his camera!

Our local newsman did get a bust shot picture of each man and had his picture on the front page, side by side, with each man's side of the story under his picture. Business was kind of slow in Lampasas about that time, and the local radio was giving the Sheriff's Office report, which all they had to report over the weekend was a drive-by cussing complaint.

Today, Lometa has a very good school with most of the community functions involving the school, or at least using the school cafetorium. We have successful sports, FFA, and Interscholastic League participants. The One Act Play has gone to state competitions several times. We have one of each: Bank, Livestock Auction, Gas station/convenience store, tire station, taxidermy, hardware, grocery, antiques, feed store, wool and mohair warehouse, senior center, Justice of the Peace, and a city hall/fire station. What more could you want? Oh yes, the two cafes and a new beer barn. The seven churches couldn't stop the beer barn. This was the first time in Lometa's history that an election legalized any form of alcohol, and I won't say any more about that.

There are several old country schoolhouses around the country that are kept up and used for an occasional community 'get-together' for ice cream or Bar B Q. There are very few that went to the school there that are still living, but some folks like me that got the history first hand enjoy passing it to the next generation. This has been the favorite way of passing on history throughout the ages all over the world. Many people care nothing about it, but thankfully, some do. Before the modern new media, news was spread by mouth from friends or strangers from biblical times to Grandpa's time on the road in front of his house, until the state built Texas Highway 183 against his wishes.

Sounds like fun living in the country, and it is, but there are many drawbacks that most people don't like or know about. First, is making a living. You just can't live off of the land like people did when they took it away from the Indians. An acquaintance of mine was concerned about a son that he had sent through college that got married, bought a few acres in Arkansas and was going to live off of the land. All that money he had spent raising the boy and sending him through college was wasted. I told him not to worry. He would soon starve out if he didn't send him any money.

I warned my bride that we might have to survive on cornbread and beans that we grew when we moved to the ranch. Young people just can't live on love very long. My first off the farm job was selling insurance, and we did eat a lot of beans and cornbread until I found out that I was not a salesman. Today, there are people that commute to work or use a computer and a phone at home to keep making a living in the country. Some have been successful at it and, some have moved back to the city.

People get spoiled into three meals a day, all kinds of entertainment, and the close at hand EMS, fireman, and police. My grandpa Ivey told me about a farmer that was going to wean his mules off of feed. About the time he got them weaned, they all died on him. People have to understand that life is just different in the country. If it is ranching they want, they need a banker that will loan them as much money as it would take to start a pretty large business anywhere. It would be harder to convince him to take on the farming business loan because the prospect doesn't have the experience or education necessary. And it does take a wide variety knowledge, techniques, and actual experience. The best advice is to look long and hard before they make the leap. Farming is one of the smallest profit margin businesses, yet it takes a terrific investment to get started.

Most people have to be able to sacrifice the good things they are used to in order to plow that little profit back into the business. That profit does not come every year. We talked about cycles. Land at today's prices will not pay for itself in a thousand years using the money it makes through agricultural enterprises. In 1942 the US Army opened Camp Hood, thirty miles East of Lometa to train solders for WWII. It has become Fort Hood and the largest land base in the free of the world. This affected the price of land by 1980 and caused many larger ranches to be split and sold. Higher taxes and the lure of wealth have made it harder for the big ranches to stay intact. Leases are about the only way, and there are many others on the waiting list for them. Off farm jobs are the most common way to be able to farm or simply live in the country.

The abundance of food in America is proven with the fact that it only takes seven to ten percent of the family income, even less if the raw food is cooked at home instead of being prepared for quick and easy meals before it reaches the grocery. Half of the courses of an Agricultural Bachelor of Sciences degree are science. All sciences are related and most are necessary to completely understand all phases of 'today's' sustainable agriculture. We use 'sound science,' not political science. The latter being the largest threat this country has to feeding ourselves and much of the rest of the world as we have in the past. Why have people from all nations in the world been trying to move to America? Cheap, healthy food and freedom! God bless America, and the farmers and ranchers.

The author and family at the Bi Centennial celebration in Lometa.

ABOUT THE AUTHOR

Travis Herring was born during the Great Depression as the third generation on a large ranch in the Central Texas Hill and Brush Country. His idol and grandfather lived just across the road and helped shape his life with stories of his experiences on the Chisholm Trail. Neighbor Jess Pickett, a black cowboy that his grandfather met on the cattle drive and made a life long friend, also contributed many stories.

These stories built a foundation for a desire to learn more about the early life of the cowboy and their adventure, fun and hardships.

Shortly after college and the army, while working with the Agricultural Extension Service in West Texas, he met a San Angelo news paper reporter, Elmer Kelton. Since they both had similar interest in stories of cowboys and early Texas, they became "Livestock show Friends" (ranch animal competitions for youth) while Travis was working with 4-H kids.

Elmer Kelton went on to become a famous Western Fiction writer, winning many awards and having movies made from some of his books, and Travis Herring went back to the ranch.

11446103R00111

Made in the USA
Charleston, SC
25 February 2012